Mission, eliminate world poverty

CHAPTER I

First meeting of the 5 men and 5 women, richest in the world;

 It will be for 3 days, counting each day with six hours of discussion of the following topics;

- What is the world to us?

- How do we see the cultures that surround us worldwide?

- What can we offer the population to have a world that meets their expectations?

- What is our legacy, which we plan to leave, to be remembered forever?

-Exhibition and union of ideas.

-Creativity and Projects.

Upon entering the exhibition hall, it shines with a great brightness, when looking to the right there is an epitaph, framed as in gold and it says;

If you died today, what a misery.

If you died today, what would you leave?

If you died today, what you still have to do.

If you died today, what would your last words be?

If you died today, what would your last wish be?

Take a deep breath and realize that life is beautiful.

You are alive, simply to give the best of you.

The life that you have belongs to you, live it with wisdom.

Let the world be a witness that you live and that you still have a lot to do.

I continue my way, we climb some stairs, we see a silver door, we enter is a splendid place, it feels a pleasant smell like rosemary and lavender that awakens all my senses. There is a large table where there are twelve seats, there is no place for the mass media, it will be a confidential meeting where we as writers will know what happens and we will have it translated into letters, the other writer I do not know, but I see that he is amazed by the beauty, the luxury that surrounds us, I observe another parchment, framed as in gold that says;

Today is the most important day of your life.

Today you are present, enjoying your senses.

Today you are the owner of this moment.

Today depends on you, if you are willing to become creative.

Today depends on you, if you become sensitive.

Today depends on you, if you feel the energy as it travels through your body.

Today depends on you, if you feel the spirit in your body, in your heart.

Today simply, today you are the owner of this moment.

Today you will transcend in the world, because yesterday is there.

Today you will transcend forever, because the future is uncertain.

We continue observing the facilities we go to a hall, full of pictures of famous painters, at the end there is a beautiful wooden door open, there is another glass door is something fantastic, a splendid garden with artificial waterfalls, butterflies, you hear the whistle of the birds, like a special song that fascinates my ears, the fall of the water is heard, as if the sounds unite and express a melody. We continue our way, all faces are enchanted, we climb a few steps, automatically opens a large door, the lights are turned on, in the center there is an orchestra that begins to play a soft melody, I feel that makes my whole body vibrate, I do not know if it is the location of the room, the architecture, but it is a sound that I had never heard and that I have attended countless concerts.

On the way to my seat, I see a giant room there are countless paintings of famous composers, there is even a sign that says "The most beautiful music in the world here you will hear". There is another parchment to the right a few steps from the room of the pictures of the transcendental composers during several eras. He says;

Music is a universal language

Each note reflects the constant struggle.

Each instrument together creates the spiritual side.

Music is life, it is energy for the soul.

Music is joy, it is nostalgia, it is love.

Music activates the senses.

Music is water in the desert.

Music is the expression that its authors are present forever.

The music reflects that out of nothing comes creativity.

Music teaches us that miracles exist.

That the impossible becomes possible in the discovery of infinity.

Music is like gold shines, but it illuminates our spirit.

We continue our way out of that great place, we enter something very bright, the light is natural as if we were outside, oh it's great, it's a gigantic aquarium, there are many white seats, I feel that softness, they give us a drink, knows how to fruit, its smell is esquicito, I am amazed by the architecture of the place, I imagine I am diving, but I can breathe well, it is a fabulous fauna, up, down, to the surroundings, we are like in a capsule or submarine , it resembles, I am amazed at the creativity, how the brain is so fabulous, that as the last parchment said, the impossible can be made possible. Imagination and wanting to do things go hand in hand, another parchment is there, it is observed as if it were inside the sea, it is inside the giant fish tank in a fabulous reef it says;

The sea is immensity.

The sea is a world still unknown.

The sea is something magnificent of creation.

The sea teaches us that what surrounds us is wonderful.

The sea tells us that knowledge never ends.

The sea tells us that every day, every moment, there is something new to know.

The constant struggle makes us find other paths.

The love of what we do, makes us like the sea, tireless.

The sea is constantly changing, its energy and immensity, are observed and felt.

The sea is beauty, it is fear, it is tempest, it is destruction.

Respecting their moods is similar to the respect of our fellow human beings.

Each person is unique, as is only what surrounds us.

The sea is inspiration, it is respect, it is energy, it is strength, it is love.

We continue our majestic path is great this place, its smell is great it feels freshness, energy at the same time, you hear an immense sound is a giant waterfall you can not hear its noise I just observe it is fantastic, I imagine touching it, but it prevents me a transparent glass, on one side there is a table in a rectangular shape with round-shaped terms are fourteen modern chairs I feel that softness, next to a panel, there is a head of ceremony announcing:

We have met this day with the only vocation to make the world remember us forever, not only for material wealth, but for the brightness that is about to emerge towards the human side, where development manifests itself as the light that illuminates hearts, the doors are open for anyone who wants to achieve success, transmitting it to society through a project that benefits the world and as a general objective, our mission, to eliminate world poverty, is very difficult, but in this life is simple nothing is given, on the contrary this life needs leaders ready to fight with courage, courage, humanism, decision, love.

We have the presence of the most outstanding leaders in the world who have impacted us with their wealth, they are the five richest men and five women in the world, today they want to go down in history as they face the most important challenge in their, his Mission, eliminate world poverty, ladies and gentlemen this is a confidential meeting for security I know they decided to change their name, but they are committed that at the end of the project we will know their full names, we give them a warm welcome I present to Mrs. Katherine, I am surprised everyone they are incorporated into their respective places, they have a golden mask their clothing is white with purple embroidery around and in the center a bright sun, Mrs. Katherine is in the luxurious panel to give her speech, colleagues from industry and business is an honor be among you with the general objective of changing the world where the welfare, the smile, the happiness, is a part of achievement for each corner, eliminating poverty we will have another vision, we will contribute leaving a trace that lasts forever, the applause sounds, the attentive head of ceremony thanks Mrs. Katherine, then Mr. Markl, head of human development, we will talk about how the contest was held to designate the twelve participants six women and six men, this project began four years ago a global call was made where it was presented, in each place, in each corner, it was given such diffusion, that there was no one who did not know about this fantastic event, the call said so;

Mission, eliminate world poverty

Throughout the present day everyone is summoned, no matter what, religion, sex, culture, social status, only that aims to help with a sophisticated project to eliminate poverty in the world.

Physical requirements;

-To have excellent health: health is very important, since physical tests will be carried out, even high performance and if you are the winner, you will travel around the world to publicize your project and should be an example to follow.

Excellent physical condition: you must practice a sport frequently and have excelled, that your physique, be athletic, during the competition you are going to submit to elite efforts, you will be given a workout, but you must have sports background.

Psychological requirements;

-You must be mentally healthy, handle your emotions properly to the place or time where you are.

-To have mental control, because you will be under constant pressure, that you will even avoid giving up.

-To be a great motivator: to take your team to success in the face of adversity

-To be a great leader: thinking forever on the human side, contribute to the development of society.

-To have a life story where difficulties have passed, where poverty has been latent, extreme suffering, where all difficulties have been overcome and become a person who is starting to succeed or who already achieved it.

Ethical and moral requirements;

-To have an exemplary conduct: according to the cultural, social standards of the world, to be a person of great education and altruistic, wise and intelligent behaviors of help to the needy.

- Honesty: Very important, honesty, knowing the responsibility that you have when presenting a great project, not having committed any crime, or having caused harm to any living being.

-Discipline: be responsible, punctual in schedules, projects, appointments, follow ideals with respect and with a goal of development, be disciplined in everything that surrounds you.

-Respect: myself and my peers, regardless of their culture, social preference, respect the slogan ¨ each person owns his life not affecting third parties to the contrary benefiting everyone who is within reach¨.

Special requirements:

-Desire of overcoming: contributing to the development of society in general, ¨don't give up in the face of challenges, however sophisticated or difficult they may seem¨.

-To want to leave a positive footprint in this world: "struggle day by day to be better, more human, wiser, more realistic, that dreams can be made reality with perseverance, determination, focus and leadership".

-Compromised with you and yours: ¨Which you walk with your head held high, that inside you know that you are capable of helping, that your project is valuable, it is more than that, it is a life project where the universe is Witness of your love, sincerity and every drop of sweat supports you with the stamp of perseverance, made with the gratification of having given the greatest effort today¨.

-That there is peace in your heart: ¨ that there is love around you, that illuminates the path of sadness, that your spirituality, happiness, achievement have been worthy of natural beauty, that your achievement brings together hearts, brilliant minds that do not stop, with a single objective to benefit those who need it most, that your powerful tools are manifested in happiness, joy and love¨.

-That your thoughts are on the horizon: ¨Your mentality must be global, not think of a few, your strategy must open infinity of hearts, that your energy is reflected more than the speed of light in the world, that your light illuminate all the existing darkness, that fill with ideas and let it be known that the impossible is usually possible¨.

This evaluation will be carried out for two years, with the best minds in the world, there will only be twelve winners, 6 women and 6 men willing to give life and soul, not only for the first place prize, but also for complying with the Mission, eliminate world poverty.

I am your server Markl, today is a great day four years were completed in which I start the project two years of the structure and two years to select the twelve winners, we will have a year on an island in the Indian Ocean, where it goes carry out an immense evaluation to find the winning project that eradicates poverty in the world and that the winner has the mentality to transmit the values of his project, that his image is of strength towards future generations, all this will be confidential Due to the fantastic nature of the project, only we are aware of our goals, objectives, achievements, which we are going to achieve for the world.

I am Markl I give my heart and soul to this project, keep silent, you hear applause full of energy, dedication, strength, the head of ceremony Anthoni, he is impatient waiting for the applause to stop sounding to intervene, thanks to Mr. Markl Boss of Human Development, today begins a great journey, our boats, are aware of the direction they are taking, our compasses indicate the essential path, but we want to look for more and we venture to know a myriad of ways to solve a global problem that is in our hands, has been a difficult road, with many obstacles, but in the end, our interest, our positive courage has come out triumphant.

We are just a short time away from history, turning the unreal into reality, finding solutions, to eliminate the suffering that poverty transmits, today the universe is witness to our project, it is something unique in life, during the history of the world never put into practice, we are aware of the constant work that is beginning to bear fruit, we have the twelve participants full of energy and attentive to the great commitment that awaits them, they are ready to start, to make history in this great contest, keep silence Anthoni and you hear some applause, please ladies and gentlemen take 30 minutes of rest we will enjoy a delicious dessert made by our magnificent chefs, the speech ends all walk to another room opens and smells delicious, I stay in the boardroom I watch Around me, as always amazed by the great luxury that surrounds me, I head towards the waterfall covered by almost natural glass, the only thing that mine the noise of the waterfall because the beauty is incomparable, surrounded by vegetation, I look to the left side, oh as I did not realize another parchment looks resplendent and says:

Miracles are like water in the desert

My wealth is not only material, my wisdom is wealth.

It was not easy to reach my goals my mind told me you can not, it's a lot for you, it's difficult.

Continue my journey with the hope of dreaming and seeing those dreams shaped in reality, someday.

There were times when I could not find an exit, I tried to go the easy way, but something prevented me from doing so.

Several people told me that it was impossible, that I did not have any illusions, they even laughed at my dreams, so I stopped counting them and I became the owner of them.

When I began to realize that miracles exist, my perspective changed, the energy returned to my body, I felt an immense heat, my face shone.

The people around me added several justifications to my success, they did not believe that miracles exist.

I surround myself with positive, spiritual, enterprising people, my life changes.

God sheltered me with a wonderful mantle full of light, where happiness surrounded me and I knew my true job of being here in this fantastic and beautiful land.

Miracles exist, because they often arrive in times of tempest, darkness, when you think there is no way out, they knock at your door.

When you feel faint, the water in the desert appears, it is the great miracle that refreshes you, that revives you, that gives you strength to continue.

In the world, only 1 percent of the population knows that miracles exist and are what will make our land a magnificent and fantastic place.

Miracles exist ...

What beautiful parchment coincides with this great room, with this great beauty, with what is happening in this place, because they do not want anyone to find out about this great meeting ?, they are afraid to fail with this great responsibility! Finally I will take out my deductions, I leave the room I go to a place that smells delicious, it is a majestic color, it is an impressive table surrounded by chefs and diners, my appetite was opened, here all the rooms are very large, I take a cake the smell, its fruity aroma and the fresh out of the oven, I start to eat it, I go around the big place several people eat, at the same time they talk, I go to have a coffee, I see a picture above a window without glass where they watch the chefs, working strenuously, they see joy, coordination, I watch the sign and it says:

The dessert and its delight

My eyes are watching you, you are magnificent.

My nose perceives you, as the most delicious.

My palate enjoys you, feeling every ingredient in my taste.

After enjoying my stomach thanks, I want more.

It is created with craft hands that give maximum effort in its preparation.

The development of a unique product, gives you personality, makes you notice before the crowds.

When you do something with love, delicacy, with greatness and determination, your spirit becomes great.

When you do what you like, when you can dedicate your life to the work in which you dream, you are in love and you are able to do it for free only for the pleasure and satisfaction.

You have crossed the barrier, to know why you are in this world.

The dessert and its delight is my letter of presentation, it is my love and my spirituality transmitted at the same time.

The dessert and its delight, fills me with motivation and emotion because I know that I contribute to be a better world.

Listen that it is wonderful to read in each place words and words that if you analyze them well, they have a great meaning, that by touching the heart they make you more spiritual, continuous, there is a giant waterfall of chocolate, the chefs provide plenty of fresh fruits, As if it were a skewer, I look like an emotional child, if I had seen this in my childhood, I think I imagine in a fairytale land, what a great place, they are giving indications that in five minutes the meeting starts again in the boardroom , I enjoy my super special skewer of fresh fruits with chocolate I continue my way, several people are entering, I'm almost done, I'm going to do it, I'm going for a chocolate, to be in my five senses attentive to the grandiosities that follow, sincerely I can not believe it if I have the privilege of being here and listening to what anyone in the world would like to know is a great privilege, I will make the most of it, I know it's something that is never going to repeat in life, I enter the beautiful room, I take my seat says mr. Richc in the badge, I feel like at my desk, go up to the grandstand Anthoni with an optimistic confident walk, his suit almost gold color distinguishes him with elegance, welcome again ladies and gentlemen, it is a wonder to find ourselves in this great place to witness of these words that are being recorded in our minds and hearts, this day is unique, we begin again the continuation of a great project that will benefit all humanity, today we are unknown all over the world, nobody knows about our meeting, but at the end of the project will know us, even in the most hidden corner of the earth will enjoy our benefits, that with the help of the entire participating population we will make this world a great community that will go down in history, where future generations will know about our seed and cultivation, they will enjoy the fruit, to continue the habit of making the project grow day by day, sound energizing applause.

Miss Laeva CEO External Integral Development and internal personality will briefly mention the profile of the twelve people who will be in the competition for the first place and the realization of their project. Collaborators, founders of this great project, we are here to present the specific characteristics of the contestants, it was a joint work, very difficult in the way of selecting the twelve, since there were lots of important works for the development , but the following personalities have given their best effort and are committed to continue, increasing their potential, because they know the great commitment that awaits them, when they meet the twelve, note that each of them has a special magic, with a altruistic spiritual sense of world character, I give by inaugurated and a great beginning of the great project, we begin;

LADIES:

1.- Name: Florencet

   Age: 28 years

   Country: Canada

   Profession: Geological Engineer

   Project: Drinking water for everyone

   Sport: Gymnast

Language: English and French

Altruism for the world: Through pure water to fulfill the primordial need.

2.- Name: Rosalinda

Age: 32 years

Country: MEXICO

Profession: Food Engineer

Project: Nourishing food for the world

Sport: Swimming

Language: Spanish, English, Japanese

Altruism for the world: create your own foods that are nutritious and enjoyable.

3.- Name: Joharim

Age: 29 years

Country: South Africa

Profession: Master in International Business

Project: Work for everyone

Sport: Cycling

Language: English, German, Portuguese.

Altruism for the world: create jobs to benefit all societies.

4.- Name: Giselle

Age: 31 years

Country: Germany

Profession: Psychologist

Project: Create a positive mindset around the world

Sport: Athletics

Language: English, German, French.

Altruism for the world: Indicate and follow up on personal strengths

5.- Name: Akeilas

Age: 34 years

Country: Russia

Profession: Doctor

Project: Health for everyone

Sport: Ice skating

Language: Russian, English, German, French

Altruism for the world: Physical and mental health to eradicate world poverty.

6.- Name: Queenie

Age: 37 years

Country: Australia

Profession: Telecommunications Engineer

Project: Avoid climate change

Sport: Swimming

Language: English, Greek, Italian

Altruism for the world: through telecommunications, create programs around the world for natural and economic wealth.

GENTLEMEN

7.- Name: Akiakv

Age: 38 years

Country: Alaska

Profession: Industrial Engineer

Project: create industries that facilitate food

Sport: Ice skating

Language: English, French, Russian

Altruism for the world: the development of industries to feed the world, with products that are easy to transport and that expire in 10 years.

8.- Name: Joao

Age: 39 years

Brazil country

Profession: Aerospace Engineer

Project: creation of construction materials

Sport: Football

Language: Portuguese, English

Altruism for the world: Collection of garbage and waste, to create resistant materials so that everyone has houses.

9.- Name: Winstond

Age: 30 years

Country: England

Profession: Chef

Project: Quality food

Sport: Rugby

Language: English, Spanish, French

Altruism for the world: Create worldwide feeding centers for the population in general.

10.-Name: Jenst

Age: 31 years

Country: Denmark

Profession: PhD in philosophy

Project: build happiness

Sport: Rugby

Language: Danish, English,

Altruism for the world: Happiness has been found to be a global need, specific objective to make organizations around the world dedicated to happiness.

11.-Name: Mahatmae

Age: 24 years

India country

Profession: Mathematical physicist

Project: lend money for creation of businesses that give employment

Sport: Yoga

Language: Hindi, English, Spanish, French, Italian, Russian, Chinese

Altruism for the world: Use creativity and innovation to encourage the population in the world to create their own jobs by providing financing to projects that have a future.

12.- Name: Ryud

Age: 27 years

Country: Japan

Profession: Electronics Engineer

Project: Harnessing solar energy

Sport: Karate

Language: Japanese, English, German

Altruism for the world: Use solar energy to eliminate poverty in the world, transport with solar energy, electricity, food.

The profile of all the finalists is great, it will be very difficult for the judges to choose the winner, they all have a great project worthy of rewarding in connection with the societies, with the biggest manifestation of the "Mission, eliminate world poverty" , on his shoulders is the indecipherable weight, of the great responsibility they have over a theme of all times, a subject that has not had a solution, a theme that only one miracle can save it, that great miracle that identifies us in this great project, where each step counts, where the soul, heart and ideas embodied in reality will be delivered, today is a great day full of challenges and incomparable support, wisdom is the only tool that can save this great project , miracles exist but you have to work and reach the maximum determination to dare to do what others have not done, that something that will make us transcend through history, through every smile, to through each sigh, through love.

Anyone in the world had the great opportunity to belong to this great group, anyone had the opportunity to see their ideas reflected, these twelve personalities are the best in the world that will make the decision to contribute to something unique, something great, which is the world development, of the individuals who need it most, thank you I am Laeva, I give as all, my heart in this great project. A brief moment of silence is heard, an energetic thunder sounds like a bomb of applause, you see the enthusiasm, the energy and the great responsibility that deserves the great project, they do not stop the applause, Mr. Richc approaches the podium the microphone wait.

Ladies and gentlemen, what astonishing it is to know all the magic of this great project and know in advance the great responsibility that runs through the veins of all the organizers, participants, mentors, teachers, creators of this great project, today is a unique day full of learning and knowledge to achieve the most important thing is wisdom, questions will arise, the importance of the confidentiality of this project, the manifestation of ideas can be stopped by negative people or without knowledge of the importance of projects that contribute development and growth, coordination is important in achieving objectives, for that reason the press is on the side, addressing it in a respectful manner that as soon as the expected results are found, an important step will be taken not only to communicate it to the media , if not everyone witnessing the effectiveness of the project, which can often be observed or imagined as an ut opía, it can be real getting the biggest miracle, where there was no alternative, we are playing our real cards of world transcendence, where we observed a desert we are willing to find water, where there was hunger, we are willing to create a clear form of structured development to eradicate world poverty, esteemed present today this day was unique and special, to work hard with a huge energy, to demonstrate that miracles exist.

At the end of the ceremony a soft music is heard that does not stop the applause, it sounds like energy, power, ability, achievement, efficiency, goals, wealth, light, it is fantastic as a song can inspire and visualize several emotions, each person retires with a great mystery, knowing the great responsibility that you have, even I feel responsible for this great project I feel it in my heart, I am with the great illusion that it is reality, there are few people in this world who really want to leave a productive footprint, I am surprised of the 10 richest in the world; 5 women and 5 men, they have exemplary lives worried about the world, it sounds sensational, unique and special, I am proud to be part of this great project, I do not like much the confidentiality of the information, I'm dying to let my family know , that everybody knows the great project, but for something they chose me and for something I am here I remember when I signed the confidentiality contract I said:

Date:

Mission, eliminate world poverty

First name:

Personal information.

I am Richc, manifested due to the selection that was made, to belong to this great group, I am aware of the danger that information runs when transmitting it, for this reason I am asked that my confidentiality be special for this project, not commenting anything, or family, friends and people outside the project, my contribution is to something very important that will have global findings, your heart, your soul, your spirit, will be left in this project, your silence is of causal benefit, your contribution is unique and special, feel proud of belonging to a family that does a great job, feel the awareness that you are in something fantastic that has never been successfully accomplished in the history of our life, it bears the responsibility, the discipline, the commitment of something unique that will transcend all times for the benefit of future generations, the concept of humanity from today runs through your veins, we are a team, we must be loyal to our team, we are the owners of the results, the world organization is the only responsible and owner of the information, the successes obtained are the responsibility of the work team, after the project of 5 years will be transmitted the information that the organism considers pertinent, as objective of the development in the world, if I agree with everything stipulated I sign in commitment.

Sincerely

As 20 signatures were on the bottom of the carefully and the contract had other sheets with small letters resembled the contracts that then signs one, that by the laziness and the inability to see the small letters, we no longer find out about the rest , finally I sign it, that's why I'm here, I feel happy, I've taken a lot of love and meaning, it's a great unique project, that comes out with the best intention, from the heart, the soul, the feelings, the spirituality, it's difficult to explain, but I feel it in my heart. Knowing how to pass the time too fast, you will already be 3 years old, in a year you have to know the winner of the 12 participants, the last year will be applicable and I do not know when the results will be given, due to the complexity is something that is not known, but I know that when those results come to light they will illuminate an infinity of hearts around the world.

I go up elevator I go to the 186 floor the triptych tells me that it is the international food area, sounds delicious, I'm quick, fast, the elevator technology is great, it's a space for 100 people, a little tight I say, but it says there is capacity for that amount, which construction God, I am amazed as technology and human knowledge has no limits, under the imposing elevator, I go to the right place, but before I see the great luxury of the place, I turn the 360 degrees, I feel vertigo because it is as if you were in heaven everything is transparent, before entering the international food hall, I see a sign, it is magnificent is not framed anywhere, it is as if they had hung from heaven, the parchment radiates light, which dazzles but does not prevent reading.

Magnificent is today

The inclemencies of the past tormented me.

It was many years ago that I fell into failure and I still relive those moments.

The pain is so strong that I still feel it, every detail is in my mind.

Today I decided, live it to the fullest, dream the real to the fullest.

Magnificent is today, it is sincere because it comes from the soul and the heart.

My thought is magnificent because I live to the fullest today.

I no longer have time to look at the past, today it is enough to fill me with joy.

Today is my life, every detail is manifested every moment.

Today is my day, I will give myself to the maximum, I will make it unique.

The pain disappeared, today is my sun, today is love, today is joy.

Magnificent is today, because it taught me that the heart today arises.

The past has died, but it gave me positive experiences like refreshing water in the desert.

I live today because I am awake, enjoying this great moment to the fullest.

I have not thought about the future, because I know that I do not own that time.

That the future may be uncertain, that the great capacity that belongs to me is the present.

I do not worry about the past anymore, magnificent is today.

Magnificent is today, because the universe is witness that I will strive at this moment.

That I will feel my steps, the air that enters my body and the flavors that encourage my palate.

Magnificent is today, magnificent is today ....

How wonderful as some simple words excite you, transport you and transform your senses, these authors of the parchment are great, they transmit real facts of philosophy and wisdom. I am transported to my past of poverty, but in reality I never considered it that way, I was very happy, well there were other things that tormented me, but since God is great, I am in this wonderful place, I am going to tell an international chef that give a pinch to know that I'm not dreaming, is that it is an immense luxury that does not pass through my mind the great astonishment that it gives me, as are the riches, of few and know that in the world there are countless people, that does not count with the essential resources.

Well for me to be sad is not the time, I have to enjoy this great moment, it is unique, wonderful, special, where the door is all transparent, I will wait for someone to arrive and I enter with the person, I did not have to wait long time when several well-dressed people arrived, elegant women and men, well, I am also elegant, my blue suit is fabulous, my silver tie looks impressive and do not tell me my shoes are very comfortable, I do not like to be presumptuous but it is I put on, an instant door opens, it is difficult to see the entrance but it seems that the people who entered have already done it several times, it resembles the place to a bubble in the sky, I observe around me there are infinity of beautiful plants, flowers, which design, smells delicious, the combination of the smell of food and the smell of vegetation is impressive.

I was shocked, as I had never taken so much into account my senses, as in this great place, since I arrived it has been amazing, I continue my way is very big space, I arrive a gentleman tells me to sit down, before he asks me for my sack and my portfolio I do it, I thank, I feel, a girl with a lot of personality comes to take my note, her eyes are special, she catches my attention, but I want to eat and enjoy the great moment, the young lady approaches me with an electronic letter, it indicates to me that I can choose, the food of the country that I want, I observe, are I imagine that the flags of the whole world or of the majority, I say that I want food from France, Mexico, select the two countries, He tells me that from France I want to show me the menu, I tell him that a salmon, a cod, selects Mexico, I tell him a barbecue with his consommé and three handmade tortillas, thank you, to drink I want a cranberry juice and a water of fruits, thank you in 20 minutes I bring your menu, I say thank you I wake up a moment, I make my usual tour, I see the fabulous kitchen chefs from all over the world working, the dining room is impressive and the diners are many, next to the kitchen there is a gigantic parchment illuminated, so that its clarity of the writing is legible and natural says:

The food in the world

Fill our palates, our senses, provide energy.

You are an art worthy of recognition, for all time you have been important.

Your characteristics start the great desire to be able to enjoy yourself.

Each step, each ingredient, complements a great process.

It is a united puzzle, each piece was selected to please the palate.

The spirituality of natural creation manifests itself in the taste.

Several populations, several people participate in a generalized process.

Food in the world is an art that involves the living and emotional state.

It is an art that carries a magnificent process that contains an infinity of hearts.

Sweat, emotion, spirituality is transmitted in the creation of products.

Life itself is amazed at the complexity of food in the world.

It is a privilege to transmit feelings with art that enter the body.

Food in the world produces energy, produces love, produces innovation.

Food in the world unites, teaches, shapes a culture, a society, the world in general.

The food in the world dreams, embellishes, enriches, integrates, relates, complements.

The food in the world is the greatest treasure that manifests itself in the elaboration.

Food in the world teaches us that whoever builds a dish builds his life.

The food in the world manifests a universal language.

The food in the world is an infinite and cultural richness.

The food in the world is fantastic, wonderful, unique and spiritual.

The food in the world is to convey the greatness of all generations.

The food in the world, the food in the world is something else.

How splendid it is to read, then enjoy the dishes you ordered and take them with great sense, with great passion, I think I'm starving, what we would do without food, I say we would die, our species would end, I arrive at my table missing two minutes for the twenty that the girl told me, oh there are they are punctual with the service, it arrives and smells wonderful, I'm going to start with Mexican food, what a wonder, the dishes are phenomenal, the French adorn them a lot they look great, That salmon is waiting for me, I love the originality of Mexican food.

When I was in Mexico it was great, it has immense, wonderful, natural, unique places, the food is great, in reality that is my vice to eat well and France is also great, the triumphal arch, its tower, the food is wonderful They serve little, but build the dish as if they were building a castle, my dishes are great, it was worth the wait, after a moment and enjoy the delicacies, the fruit juice, I am satisfied, it is important to meet the main needs of each individual, I feel like new with more energy, it is an immense satisfaction I feel ready for what comes, I leave the place so nice, I walk towards the great elevator, I go out to the ground floor I would like not to retire I feel a little nostalgia, because I'm leaving this great place, what are the wonders that people of high economic status can enjoy, I imagine that they no longer appreciate them as much as I am doing or com or anyone who had never been in a place like this would observe it as a dream, under the big elevator, I was approached by a person who says to me. Richc I am your server Arturs who will take you to the airport, I am headed to a great limousine, what service, I am amazed as they treat us very great.

CHAPTER II

I continue my way in this luxurious vehicle, it indicates to me in a board that in 46 minutes we are in the airport, I observe in front a screen a control to select the menu, they are infinity of writings, I am going to select this one, its title is;

Positive thoughts

It is complicated in the storm to have positive thoughts.

It is worth having an active mindset towards positive thoughts.

The seed that you sow in your mind will grow, over time it will bear fruit.

Your cultivation has to go in the way of several stages, time will be witness.

Your perseverance will be noticed, it will be the mirror that reflects your battles.

Your achievements will fill you with energy, ready for the next encounter.

Your failures will provide you with teaching, experience will be the key to the right path.

Your positive thoughts will create roots, which will give you strength in the storm.

You will seek the greatest treasure that is wisdom, knowledge in its greatest greatness.

Storms will appear, but your positive thoughts will be the sun that will bring them down.

Your work day by day will bear fruit, your cultivation will be the reflection of your effort.

Your dedication, your love for what you do will give you happiness.

Positive thoughts will give you a special and unique personality.

Your relationships will have the power to create the exact spiritual bond of love.

Your positive thoughts will be the garden with the best variety of flowers.

The foundations of your life will be reflected by a special shine on your way.

Your energy will be exposed in each project, at each moment.

The present will be a matter of constant struggle without waiting for the result.

When the greatest miracle comes, enjoyment will be the reward.

Simply positive thoughts are the basis of growth.

Feel that you can change your life in a positive way.

The ties that led you to climb mountains, you have to keep building.

Future generations have to continue the path.

Your legacy will not be followed exactly, but it will have life similarities.

Your positive thoughts will improve your profile, guide you in the dark.

Your positive thoughts are light for life.

Your positive thoughts are fuel for your body.

Your positive thoughts are spiritual greatness.

Your positive thoughts, you are the owner, you know if they will transcend.

Your positive thoughts will contribute in your formation to success.

Your positive thoughts are the soul of your body.

Your positive thoughts are a great gift of the universe.

What a magnificent thought, really that when you find yourself in situations where there is no way out, motivation is necessary to find solutions and answers to our problems, it is almost 8 o'clock at night I am going to travel in the dark, I love to travel for the day, to observe the places, I enjoy traveling but observing clearly what surrounds me, Arturs stops, comes towards me, mr. Richc, before we get to the airport you're going to put on a mask so you do not look at the place, you know what the policies are like on the big event, if Arturs, if you give confidentiality, puts a sleeping mask on me, I lie down and Arturs continues on his way.

I think about everything that is being formed, the great group that I belong to, the great responsibility that we all have, the great confidentiality with which it is being handled, will give many benefits, since it is important to bring to light the great project in when you have the winner and start to find the expected results, Arturs stopped, sir, the mask can be removed, we arrived, we are on a lonely track and with a magnificent jet ready to depart, its great design impacts a white color with golden paint that adorns it, inside is very luxurious I had never seen anything like it, there are only two more people and the staff of the jet, are I imagine, that also amazed at the great luxury, I say good night they answer me, I take my seat , the assistant tells me to use the safety belt, take off, tell me if I want something, tell him that a little water only, a relaxing music starts playing, it's great to travel in this technology, no movement feels, compared to commercial airplanes, I relax, I do not know how many hours we are going to travel, I fall asleep, I wake up and open the window, there is the immense sun, I look at the front, I see a parchment that is like a small golden box with a dim and bright light.

The sky

Wonder of nature, when I look at you, I think.

Your formations make me imagine different scenarios.

Your notes soften my walk.

Your brightness transmits harmony and peace.

Sky, I am amazed because you are one of the many wonders of the universe.

Birds are privileged because they feel your touch, feel your strength.

The sky adorn the earth gave light and beauty.

Your immensity to see you is infinite.

Your rain refreshes, your rain is life.

Heaven gave me inspiration.

When I see you I feel the energy, I raise my dreams, my thoughts grow.

I rejoice in you when I look for alternatives or solutions.

The sky filled my heart with light, the sky filled my heart with joy.

Heaven simply gave me the inspiration I needed.

What detail, I analyze every thought, it's great what a few simple words can do, they transport you, you feel emotion, like I already have an appetite, I press a button, the assistant asks for a saucer and a juice, it's wonderful to be in the clouds enjoying of food, where we arrive will be the main meeting point of competitors to transport us to the place where we will be a year, until the winner comes out, anyone would say it is too long, but the reality is that time passes quickly, when we least expect them we will have the expected results and a little more, I know that miracles exist, because of the great plan I know that they will obtain the best results, they announce that we have reached our destination, I lost the notion of time I do not know how many hours we flew, I decided not to use a clock, to take my time without pressure, but I love watches, only this time I made the exception. Under the plane there is a gigantic surprising room, in the shape of a u, way to go around the place where the participants arrive, in the room of the jets there is an impressive sign that stands out:

Faith

It is something spiritual that materializes our dreams.

It is the one that has moved all the great projects in the world.

The faith that in times of storm is the only solution.

The faith that is the key to the unknown.

The universe is witness to your power.

You came to me when failure appeared, I did not lose faith.

When the impossible exists, only faith makes it possible.

Faith is like fresh water in the desert.

Faith has witnessed the wonderful worldwide advances.

When there have been no alternatives, acts of faith have appeared.

Faith is something great, it is in the heart.

The sincere manifestation is light in the dark.

The beauty of faith is seen in achievement, in determination.

Faith is reality, when you imagine where this is a dream.

Faith moves the world, moves the soul and hearts.

When the problems grew and there was no way out the faith appeared.

Your emotions, your motivation went hand in hand with faith.

Faith simply helped me believe and be in the fantastic place that I am.

Faith taught me that the world is something great.

The world is made of an infinity of amazing creations.

Faith in the ruins taught me its power.

Faith gave me a productive life.

Faith gave me sensitivity to what surrounds me.

Every day that passes I am amazed that everything is done with faith.

Faith has fulfilled the dreams of countless people.

Faith is love, wonder, something unique.

Faith is everything.

This wonderful epitaph is exact, I believe that I am living a dream, I do not believe I am in these great places, every day that passes I am more amazed, the faith is wonderful, it helped me to be here making my dreams come true, they are already coming down from another jet participants, come to the meeting point, you notice some worried, but it is normal who will not be nervous with this great responsibility that is carried on the back, it is a gigantic commitment, something that nobody has done, maybe what They have tried, but it has been unsuccessful.

The "Mission, eliminate world poverty" is an act of faith that will be carried out with the greatest possible work, the intervention of the best minds in the world, can make this dream a reality, make true the greatest miracle that is to eradicate poverty. where there is a lot of sadness for the basic issues, that becomes joy, hope, get ahead and make a mark in this world, in order to continue with work, I approach we meet, a uniformed military man, a suit great with countless decorations, is rising to the platform.

Ladies and gentlemen welcome, to this great global project in which your intervention will be important, for the life of our planet of future generations, I am the commander of special forces Brusche, I will be in charge of your security and unique indications, that will help them to their formation, we will be an effective work team with the same goal of world development, it is a difficult path that is presented, the great responsibility that each one has, is to give more of his capacity, the maximum effort will be your philosophy, responsibility, discipline, honor will be worthy representatives of your project, we are reunited with the same objective of transcending before the current population and future generations, it is specific to generalize that the success of the project depends on us, we will manage the conditions necessary for our dream to be fulfilled.

The honor, the responsibility will be constant in our minds, I will take care of taking them on a sophisticated path that gives them the parameters of real life, the learning they will get will be practical, to know what to do in times of crisis, in issues of short times with the greatest efficiency, discipline and responsibility, I am not alone we have a great team that will coordinate your training, we will make a great working union, because you will complement the learning, with your experiences and your free will, mutually we will help, because it is a project where responsibility is the main factor, all of us who are part of this group, are responsible for the positive results we will obtain from this great experience.

We will all contribute to create our great global structure that will serve the population for its development, each of you has an infinity of experiences, we will generate a single positive knowledge that supports our structure, we are all a single project, open people that will retire, but they will know how to leave the necessary roots to know that they were and belonged to this great project, fight with the soul, the heart, that the force, the energy unite them, so that this project prototype continues to bear fruit in many generations, that the arrangements that are made, to expand knowledge, for the benefit of future generations.

I am proud to belong to a great group that is distinguished by its projection towards the future, its families, the population in general, needs to observe in you an example to follow, a generalized imitation of what they do for the good of the community, I have been in countless projects risking my life, offering my country, my family, my efforts, no goal, no goal was easy, all required my greatest effort, I am willing to give my life for this great project, we are gathered to leave footprint in this wonderful world, we are willing to make the best effort, every day, every minute, every second, the present is our ally, we depend on future results, I ask only that they be delivered to the maximum today, in this instantly, the results obtained will be reflected not only on the outside, but also in the interior, where many times we do not know that place, I invite you to feel happy and proud I belong to this project, I welcome you, your families, the representation of your country, which you carry not only in your mind but in your hearts.

¨ I am willing to give my life in this moment, my dedication, my discipline, my honor, my effort will be witnesses to the great project that I belong, I have sown the seed, I am taking care every moment to obtain the best harvest, that I will transmit around of the world, physically, spiritually and universally ". Thank you.

Sounds of applause with a huge energy, transmitting, motivation, emotion, joy, sense of belonging, is a great project, which so emotional welcome, I left two tears of emotion die, but I observe that I am not the only sentimental, there is more people, it is a project that reaches the heart, I do not know if it will be due to time, to the greatness of the project, but It Is a great pride to belong to this great group, I say that by joining countless minds with the same purpose our lives they are going to change in a positive way, because we wish with great faith that all the population in the world receives the benefits of the sophisticated project, each one of our hearts, thoughts, soul, spirituality, are here. Commander Brusche is still on the platform, ladies and gentlemen, please, I am going to mention the list of the 12 competitors starting with the women, as soon as the names are raised, they raise their hands and get on the first plane:

Ladies

1.- Florencet, Geological Engineer

2.- Rosalinda, Food Engineer

3.- Joharim, Master in International Business

4.- Giselle, Psychologist

5.- Akeilas, Doctor

6.- Queenie, Telecommunications Engineer

Gentlemen

7.- Akiakv, Industrial Engineer

8.- Joao, Aerospace Engineer

9.- Winstond, Chef

10.- Jenst, Doctor of Philosophy

11.- Mahatmae, Mathematical Physicist

12.- Ryud, Electronics Engineer

Welcome to the great project to this great journey, to this great journey, I continue with the great privilege of mentioning the following crew members of the next plane, they are the structure that will lead the way of learning and wisdom to our competitors, these are their ten teachers;

1.- Laeva, CEO Integral external and internal personality development

2.- Noetherli, Director specializing in human development, Bioenergetics and healing sports.

3.- McYuretzili, Scientist investigations in human behavior

4.- Curielm, Scientist, Philosopher, Psychologist.

5.- Yessica, Sports Trainer Special Forces

6.- Markl, Head of Human Development, studies in Genetic Engineering

7.- Vincir, Scientist, Doctor of Human Development Sciences

8.- Teslac, Scientist, Philosopher, Inventor, studies on religions

9.- Edisonic, Psychologist, Philosopher, Doctor in International Business, Strategic personality studies of the best leaders in the world.

10.-Salomomr, Sports Coach Special forces, Psychologist, research in business development with the influence of sport.

With the special collaboration of Mr. Richc; Professor, Psychologist, motivator, writer. Her main job will be to observe and document together with Professor Aracelint; Chef, Administrator, Psychologist, Human Development Research, ready to write the great story, welcome to creativity and innovation that will witness the great project that is about to change the world in a positive way, with the only union of a Only thought "Mission, eliminate world poverty".

We went to the next plane that luxurious, beautiful and great are, again I repeat that this is something unique, I do not like much that we do not talk with my colleagues, but it is correct, the contributions we make among us will be made a week before, that the first competitor is eliminated, each month one will be discarded, that is, one week before we will make the comments and the corresponding evaluations, to know who we are going to withdraw from the competition, this work is difficult, but the reality that the benefits will be unique and the transcendence will be special, I do not know where they take us, but we are already starting, I look out the window and I see the competitors' plane aside, we are going to leave almost at the same time, I am among the best teachers in the world, I notice them thoughtfully, it is a very strong responsibility is reflected in their faces, I imagine they feel like me, as in a dream, but at the same time with a great responsibility, but that in life is easy, I see a screen in front of me, there are countless digital scrolls in it, I put on my headphones, I press the button, I select;

Dreams

I see you and I can not believe it, I play and I'm awake.

They were times of uncertainty, where reality disappeared.

The fantasy era ran through my mind.

Not finding an exit, I forgot to dream.

I believed that dreams did not come true.

I look back and see that the past is there.

That I own this instant called present.

That my strength and my energy return because I no longer think about the future.

I let myself be carried by the current, making the most of the day.

I own this moment, the past was about learning and experience.

The past only remains for me to rescue the good, the positive.

Dreams came to my mind with such freshness with a special aroma.

I do not own the future anymore, I do not think about it anymore, I just let myself go.

My frustrations have disappeared, I only think at this moment that it is mine.

Dreams finally come back from that abyss of sadness and darkness.

The light has reached my heart, I am blissful and privileged.

I have no worries, I think in the moment, the past is behind.

I do not own the future.

I will try my best at the moment, which is the path that belongs to me.

Dreams, the only thing I know, I will give my best effort, in my lapse of time.

I am the owner of this small moment, I am going to deliver, the soul, my energy, my enthusiasm, to achieve my dreams.

In this simple instant I will be wonders, I will fulfill my dreams.

Dreams that magnify my path, that give me alternatives.

Dreams that walk beside me without thinking about them.

I feel light, the heavy load has disappeared, I feel fantastic.

I have regained my strength, my vision is in this moment, I am happy.

Fate has given me this fleeting and unique moment.

Dreams that arrive without asking for them.

Dreams that appear in my mind with the magic of light that fills my being.

Dreams that not asking for them appear in own will.

Dreams that lead me down the path of miracles.

Dreams that give me joy, love, spirituality, understanding.

Dreams that come true without imagining it.

Dreams that appear out of nowhere, your reality amazes me I know I'm awake.

Dreams that I imagine to be sleeping, dreams that show me that miracles exist.

Dreams that originated an invention until it became reality.

Dreams that are real, even if they look like dreams.

What a beauty my God, this is something great and the music that was heard with the thought was great, I feel nostalgic with the desire to mourn, is that this scroll conveys my reality, I feel that I am in a dream, in a great dream, unique and special. My life is a dream come true, if God told me that at this moment I die, I would appreciate how lucky I have been, that my life has been a great dream, that I have taken my achievements as a unique miracle, I consider myself very fortunate , sometimes I feel that in this life I have received more than I deserve, I come from a family, we were not rich but we never missed anything, I begin to think that it must be difficult that you do not have the necessary resources to lead a normal life, a life with joys, with love, I feel nostalgic and I know that I will respond to the maximum in this great project, you hear a statement from the booth, ladies and gentlemen, teachers, my greatest appreciation and gratitude for the great adventure they were willing to begin, please put on all the headphones I will give you an intimate, spiritual message, mentally show you the characteristics of the great place that you will live for a year, sounds a relaxing music sigh.

I am Mr. Einsteinlci, I speak on behalf of my nine colleagues committed to the sophisticated project, our lives have not been easy, someday they will know our true stories, that it was not easy, to reach the place where we are, our commitment is not to seek the success, that path we already know, what we want is to unite the hearts, spirits, minds, to achieve a single goal, all of us that have been in this project since we started, we are leaving a hard to erase footprint, in our project we do not there are only our minds there is something else where the universe is the only witness, to observe them I see their commitment, their ethics, their determination, they know that they are belonging to something important that will transcend their lives, their soul, their hearts, we help without asking anything to change, only the faculty of effort, the dedication of the members and the world in general, we know that an idea is a light, that if it joins more ideas, the light is so wonderful that the darkness is eliminated, our good intentions are placed in their respective places, the greatness of our ideas will be transmitted from individual to individual, nation after nation, to make a single language of creativity, innovation, strength, courage , to defend our project against adversity, our free will has united in a single idea our war title ¨Mission, eliminate world poverty¨.

An extensive, difficult, complicated path, where the attempt has been made, but without good bases, we have united together with the brilliant minds, to open the chapter of solving the problem of all times, we have united to be creative and find the link that many consider lost, to unite that chain, that circle of strength that will unite us forever, between failures and adversities, that dreams can become reality, that it is simply to believe, work, propose, return to work, unite creative ideas, return to work, someday there will be rest, when we least expect it, that rest will be to relive the trophy of what we have achieved, with such effort, that the rest will be reliving day after day, the success of our great project.

Teachers are in a great project you know, there is a lot of responsibility, but there is also a lot of recognition, we are doing what countless people have never dared through the times, we know that we are intelligent, but we also know that we have an extra capacity unknown, today is the time to bring out all our experience, all our knowledge and our greater ability to do more than we think, to deliver to the maximum is not enough, we must add more of our own, more of our humanity, more than our spiritual sense, to see that we are warriors willing to die in battle, giving what we have the most and much more, is for us a pride that belong to our work team, we are a single union with the same objective, the universe is a witness of our good intentions, of our transcendence, that when we do not find a way out and the greatest thing in life appears, a miracle, I look for it we care with perseverance, with determination, courage, energy, strength, spirituality, love.

Ladies, gentlemen, be welcome, I leave you with this video to analyze where they are going to be, they will have the best facilities, I will attach the information, according to the study of your profile and your recommendations, if you want more things that are added simply ask for it . They will be a bit lonely, but among you they will be able to comment on the progress according to how they are organized.

Mr. Einsteinlci ends, what speech we have heard is transmitted with sincerity, from the heart or the soul, it is something great, I am observing it is a great place, it is a fortress, all the luxuries, that we had not imagined are in that place, in that aspect we will be very well, there is something written, please when arriving at the place they will be given more information, what extra information they will give us everything looks spectacular, it is an Island, where it will be located, it is difficult to know it is an Island giant with its own airport, but from what I see only we will be in that place, it is perfect, to do our work in the best way, what emotions will transmit the competitors, if we, we are that we can not believe this great journey, I imagine that are impacted and see nervous, because of the great competition that awaits them, we are unique in life, we agree on some feelings but in the end, everyone has their criteria, how beautiful I am lodge relaxes me and at the same time makes me think, I know I'm in a wonderful project, we will all contribute with our grain of sand and the extra that we are willing to add, we know that in life the roads are difficult, that falls many times they teach to awaken from your comfort zone, in these cases commitment and discipline are important, many people in the world depend on the success of this project, we are all nervous and we know the great responsibility, due to the dimension of the project they are going to take the competitors too many days to find the true link that completes, the chain of achievement, the chain of success, we are arriving, from the cabin they mention us that we are about to land, I observe the Island, I believe it is a private island, but it is very large from up here you can see its sophisticated form, it has roads, lakes, buildings, it looks like a country that has all the services and a little more.

From here you can see the wonderful place that we are going to explore, that will witness creativity, exchange of ideas and innovation, the plane stops to indicate that we can descend, what emotion I feel as if I were going to step on the moon for the first time, what a wonderful feeling, I'm going down the stairs of the plane, it breathes fabulous, a pure air enters my lungs, with a special smell of fresh vegetation, I feel like the sun penetrates my skin, its energy that is transmitted to my body, we get on a bus that takes us to the aviation terminal, the bus enters through a tunnel too illuminated we travel approximately 2 minutes, we are in a spectacular place, since we get off the bus, Commander Brusche is heading towards us, along with him there are several people women and men with a spectacular physical appearance, all wear military uniform, the commander tells us with a strong, confident, motivating voice;

Dear participants and collaborators, today is a unique day we are gathered to go down in history, we are warriors ready to help the world to build it, to benefit the most needy population, I, Commander Brusche, together with my work team are willing to offer our lives for this great cause, we are in charge of their safety, at all times we will be watching that everything goes in the best way, my team is the best in the world, are willing to die if necessary in compliance with our duty, today they change their lives, it is a unique and special adventure that will transcend through history, they will be remembered the great moments we spend together, each person owns their own history, but our union and strength will keep the energy, the light, of being a single force, that the impossible, we make it reality, with discipline, the greatest effort, dedication, that each ideal that runs through our veins is united in only one, so that this community, arises before the storms, before the adversities, before the fear, I welcome you again, this will be your winner's house for a year, the participants that have to leave this great place, I ask you that they surrender all their power, so that they leave a trace that is indelible forever, they have just stepped on a place, a war field of ideas that are going to transcend through history, all the brilliant minds present collaborate for a single cause, feel committed to fight to the end, that every drop of sweat, be joy for their hearts, when they feel faint, mentalize the great responsibility they have on their backs, which is a benefit project for the population of the whole world, which that they obtain in this great place will never be repeated, live each day as if it were the last, every day is unique and special, their families will feel proud of you, for the great step of transformation world, that their names are going to be written in history, warriors are welcome to your home, worry for you, for giving your best, for transcending, for external control to be followed literally and my team will be in charge, open opportunities that do not observe us, but there we will be invisible to you, but with the greatest value, to protect them to the fullest, be welcome.

You hear applause that thunder of emotion, that speech, I have noticed that until now all discourses carry soul, spirit, courage, motivation, heart, are great motivators, they reach us deep in our hearts, you see in your face of competitors, hunger and the desire to stand out, to contribute, to a better world.

The commander speaks, at the moment, we will transport them to their new homes follow me please, we go out through a golden door that opens automatically as at 50 meters there are 3 gigantic helicopters, they are lit the noise is very loud, it looks like a movie of science fiction, we all climb, the competitors introduce them in a special plane, we go together as if we were in a parade, three helicopters at the same pace as soul mates, from up here you see everything spectacular is an earthly paradise, full of lakes, waterfalls, vegetation I say that for the beauty and the essential conditions there must be wild animals, we are descending to a fortress, it is a castle all in white, it shines, in the middle of the sun, like a robust diamond that stands out in the midst of beauty , everything around resembles me to the paradise mentioned by the religions or biblical texts, we are going down towards the great castle, it is very big and has a wall around which and encloses it as a unique jewel.

We get off the helicopters and at the moment they retire, it is a fabulous place inside a river with waterfalls, it has luxury yachts, sports area, Olympic swimming pools, gyms with transparent glass, it is observed as if the gyms were out in the open, I am stunned, it is a place of luxury, here the pretexts are not going to exist because we have a unique comfort zone, we are entering the castle, outside it looks like in fairy tales, it has a spectacular architectural design, It will never be out of fashion, I know it will always be a modern work, inside it is full of immense luxury, I say that it is made entirely of marble or a very luxurious material, which will always stand out, there are plenty of art, paintings of recognized artists, it looks like a museum, with the best works in the world, there is a fabulous parchment in the center, I am sure that its surroundings are pure gold, it shines with immensity, he says;

Art inspires me

A work of art is a legacy in the world.

An essential trace of history.

The mind speaks demonstrating its creativity.

The mind speaks by expressing what the heart says.

Art inspires me, it produces eternal spirituality.

Out of nowhere was born the idea, where countless minds did not observe anything.

Each individual sought an alternative none emerged.

Years passed, the decades, the poor field was enriched.

With an idea ready to grow and be born in the arid soil.

Art inspires me, gives my life meaning.

Out of nothing came an idea that he never believed in.

This idea was embodied in a fact that seemed to be from another world.

It was demonstrated and the universe witnessed great creativity.

The miracle arose, nothing disappeared.

Art inspires me, the universe is witness to immensity.

Where the imagination was not, a seed grew that flourished.

I lost control of myself, I disappeared from the earth, to inspire myself in creation.

I knew that I am unique in life, that my mind should be spiritually creative.

When I woke up and saw my creation, I did not think it was the owner.

Art inspires me, I was like a puppet before creation.

The source of my inspiration was uncertain, it was something unique.

My work of art can never be repeated, because the time was unique.

The demonstration was unique, I will never know how I did it.

But I know it's something unique, where I was the transporting mind of the universe.

Art inspires me, as it was I do not know, I watch the work and I know I did not do it.

It was something else a strange power that manifested itself, in full bliss.

The gift he receives from manifesting my feelings and emotions without knowing it.

Masterpiece I turn you to see and I know that I was only an instrument for creation.

Many believe that I am the author, but it was someone else who enlightened me.

Art inspires me, I believe that miracles exist.

Art inspires me, I believe in the extraordinary things that happen in life.

Art inspires me, that I do not own creation, that it belongs to someone else.

Art inspires me, to live life to the fullest, enjoying every special moment.

Art inspires me, art inspires me, art inspires me to be better every day.

What beauty of poem is felt in the heart, motivates to realize all the dreams, desires and goals that we have in mind, this scroll to read it transmits positive energy, what a wonder, we are gathered in the center of the castle, what a luxury, my God, all what can be done with creativity and money, tell us to go to the spectacular elevator, it is very large says capacity 100 people, it is completely glass, we are all with astonishment, it shows in the faces, we go up very fast we are, on the 29th floor, we leave the elevator, we are in a hallway that leads us to a room, this is a fortress, we enter through a door that opens automatically to our step oh that room, this is too much luxury, I believe that the stories of fairies and princesses would be amazed by this great place, it smells great, it is a combination of unique, fresh, relaxing aromas, the living room is huge.

We go to a conference room everything looks great, as if there was nothing around, only those glasses that are invisible barriers to each place, have the most sophisticated and current technology that I have observed, we are in a room where the furniture is placed in the center of the panel u, the lights go out, a bright light appears in the center, a shadow appears that stands out with a golden garment that shines in the darkness, goes up to the panel the lights come on, a spiritual voice is heard but with energy penetrates the ears, I am your servant Taoci spiritual Guru, I do not come to talk about religion, but the spiritual sense runs through my veins, I am to protect them from the negative energy, which is on our planet, I am ambassador of peace , of wisdom, of light, of the constancy of positive energy, that we will develop to the fullest in this great project.

When you feel lonely, destroyed, desperate, I will be there to eliminate the heavy burden of negative thoughts, today this day, forget fear, the construction of your life is left to my charge, count on my unconditional support, you can call me your friend , your brother, as your heart expresses it, at this moment all my knowledge belongs to you, all the wisdom that I have obtained through time, it is yours, the universe is witness that my contribution will be for your benefit, so that they reach their objectives and expected goals, I am the light that illuminates them in the dark time, I am the calm after the storm, I am joy, I am love, I am spirituality, I am your support, I am your voice, I am to listen to you, Make your stay here unique and enjoyable.

This path that you chose, is full of challenges, strengths, weaknesses, commitment, discipline, motivation, creation, innovation, knowledge, self-knowledge, plans, strategies, dreams, miracles, love, I know that you have wounds that come dragging as if they happened in this instant, Karma or the law of cause - effect, as you want to call it, has to arm itself in a positive way, so that it is in your consciousness, like the feedback you need, to emerge in the discovery of yourself and your surroundings, Today on this day you are born again your contribution will go down in history, your spirit will be around the world, born of the soul and the heart. These words that I am going to express are in the depth of my heart, but it is an energy that I can not stop needing to hear it, please listen to it with the soul, the heart, with the whole body, it says so;

Universe

How small I feel before your greatness.

Many questions interact through my mind essentially thinking Who am I?

There are countless answers, but none of them reaches my heart.

My soul and my spirit are hungry for knowledge, wisdom, experience.

Sometimes I worry about me, it's a feeling, where sadness disappears.

Joy flourishes, the greatness that I observe is original, it is unique, it is not material.

I feel small before your greatness, with the interest to know more.

Find the most precious treasure that is wisdom, reason for life.

My mind spreads, it extends seeking peace, understanding and reflection.

My biggest wish is to grow a seed that reaches every corner.

That this fruit be enjoyed, that is the goal fulfilled, the fulfillment.

Magnificent universe, that you are infinity of answers, I take you in me, I am in you.

Your complexity makes me stronger, gives me several reasons for meaning of my existence.

You gave me this body that I often do not know.

You gave me spirituality, the one that takes me to the most hidden places.

I am a warrior at your disposal, I give you my life to benefit humanity.

Every tear that has passed through my face has been the freshness of sincerity.

My human side grows, because material wealth is not a whole.

There is something else that gives meaning to my place in this world.

I come to give the best of me, because life is short.

Every message I receive teaches me that life is wonderful.

The challenges that come my way, my falls, my failures, will make me stronger.

Because my life is unique and unrepeatable, it is a movie where I am the protagonist.

Where the sources of knowledge await me in the great mountain of wisdom.

The experience I get will help me have fewer failures or get out faster.

Universe the complexity of my understanding will give me tools of struggle.

My human side grows, the sensitivity is in me, feelings bloom.

The scars closed, spirituality helps me face that past.

The storms invaded me, but then the sun shone.

I observed my treasures, I realized that I am fortunate.

What I thought had no value, enriches me.

I value the present, because the past gave me experience and learning.

I own this moment I can do what I want, I have free will.

The future is uncertain, it does not belong to me.

In this moment of time, I will fight with strength, that my legacy will be observed day by day.

May my pride be reflected in constant struggle, courage, discipline.

That my life has meaning in my well-being and benefit of the beings that surround me.

I will go down in history as the person who fought with courage, perseverance, who never gave up.

Universe your magnitude is unpredictable, to understand you I have to be spiritual.

My goal is to turn on the light of the heart, of all the individuals that want a change.

That change that produces smiles, love and happiness.

That change that gives a meaning to their lives in synchronization with the universe.

Universe your greatness surprises me, I know you are to observe my feelings.

I know you are here to know that I need the wisdom necessary to transcend.

Each tear teaches me the true feelings.

My emotions sigh, for true love.

I am alive, aware of my contribution to the universe.

I am willing to give my life, as an offering and light of the universe.

Universe, universe, universe, universe, universe.

Give me life and energy to show you what I am.

A warrior capable of fighting for happiness, hope and love.

I am Taoci, your spiritual friend, willing to follow up and solve your constant fears, to the magnificence of life, to the enjoyment of this great moment. I see around me they are applauses that come from the heart, I am not the only one who cries, all faces are full of tears, but they are special tears that transmit energy, sincerity and love, the guru Taoci retires, his presence shows spirituality, a transportation to the non real, all the lights go on, I am Aracelint, at this moment, this is your house, every month one of you will leave this place.

Start a projector to show us the images on a screen, they will have 12 houses that have been made so that you have the best luxury and comfort, each one has a modern study center, they have a special chef to Each one of you, massage area, sauna, a private hospital, yoga area, meditation, a pool by house, Taoci guru is in this mountain, someday you will know the reason for its location and infinity of things that you will know about according to your request, I inform you that when there are only six participants will change residence to this castle that they see around them, here on the screen I show them the weekly schedule for four weeks, each month will change, as each one will have the physically , for analysis and understanding;

Monday	Teacher	Subject
8:00 a.m. to 10:45 p.m.	Salomomr	Physical and mental training I
11:00 to 12:45	Laeva	Global Leadership I
12:50 to 13:50	FOOD	
14:00 to 15:45	Teslac	Innovation I
16:00 to 17:45	McYuretzili	Communication and understanding I
18:00 to 18:55	Edisonic	Transcendental Ideas I
19:00 to 20:00	Noetherli	Yoga Bioenergetics I

Tuesday	Teacher	Subject
8:00 to 10:45	Salomomr	Sports Philosophy and Training I
11:00 to 12:45	Markl	Human Development I
12:50 to 13:50	FOOD	
14:00 to 15:45	Vincir	Creatividad I
16:00 to 17:45	Curielm	Motivation I
18:00 to 18:55	Yessica	Positive mentality I

19:00 to 20:00	Noetherli	Yoga Bioenergetics I

Wednesday	**Teacher**	**Subject**
8:00 a.m. to 10:45	Yessica	Training special forces I
11:00 to 12:45	Laeva	Global Leadership I
12:50 to 13:50	FOOD	
14:00 to 15:45	Teslac	Innovation I
16:00 to 17:45	McYuretzili	Communication and understanding I
18:00 to 18:55	Edisonic	Transcendental Ideas I
19:00 to 20:00	Noetherli	Yoga Bioenergetics I

Thursday	**Teacher**	**Subject**
8:00 to 10:45	Salomomr	Sports Philosophy and Training I
11:00 to 12:45	Markl	Human Development I
12:50 to 13:50	FOOD	
14:00 to 15:45	Vincir	Creatividad I
16:00 to 17:45	Curielm	Motivation I
18:00 to 18:55	Yessica	Positive mentality I

| 19:00 to 20:00 | Noetherli | Yoga Bioenergetics I |

Friday	**Teacher**	**Subject**
8:00 a.m. to 10:45	Salomomr	Physical and mental training I
11:00 to 12:45	Markl	Communication I
12:50 to 13:50	FOOD	
14:00 to 15:45	Vincir	Creatividad I
16:00 to 17:45	Curielm	Motivation I
18:00 to 18:55	Yessica	Positive mentality I
19:00 to 20:00	Noetherli	Yoga Bioenergetics I

Saturday	**Teacher**	**Subject**
8:00 to 17:45	Salomomr	Training Exploration Forces
	Yessica	Specials I
18:00 to 20:00	Noetherli	Yoga Bioenergetics I

Sunday

Strategic rest; with work options according to the needs of the participant.

Important note:

All the subjects are focused, with the project of each competitor.

This is the great schedule, which will guide your paths, today is Sunday relax, mentalize, for the day tomorrow you will need all your available energy, please board the bus that will take you to your new homes enjoy this beautiful and magnificent place , have a great day, I am Professor Aracelint again welcome you to this new home.

We retire is magnificent, the matters with which the great group will count and the important thing is that I will be part of their team, I will take the classes, I will be at the expectations of what happens, we get on the luxurious bus, the technology is magnificent and the beauty around us of this island, are modern communication ways, with the unique nature that characterizes it, counts the road with an almost invisible fence, behind you can see an infinity of fauna and flora, beautiful waterfalls, crystalline lakes of blue color turquoise, what beauty my eyes perceive is something unique, a jewel, a treasure that can not be observed anywhere, we are in an earthly paradise.

We arrived at the right place is a fabulous architectural structure, everything is futuristic, had never been in a place like that, the combination resembles a dream, with the unique and special nature that is here. We got off the luxurious bus, what a wonderful place, each one of us has our own house, in each house there is a name shining like gold, this great detail makes us special, there is my house, says Mr. Richc, they tell us that we can go to our houses, we read the documentation that is on our desk, I observe some faces of amazement of the competitors, since I have seen them, they keep their expressions the same, is that this experience we are living is unique and incomparable, we said goodbye Each and every one enters his house, the entrance door is fabulous, everything is luxury around me, everything is modern, my favorite area the office is very big made with some great glass, I have a 360 degree view, I have a view towards a lake, towards the forest, towards the mountains, it is the place that I have always dreamed of, it is a place that produces inspiration, any writer, I would take this place as a spiritual center of learning, practice and meditation.

Under the stairs, the kitchen is splendid there is a computer, I will read the instructions, to what good, I can eat what I want and someone will bring it to me, says an important note, everything you consume here is the freshest and healthiest of the world, your food is our responsibility, well, with such a great diet, you have to come up with complementary ideas for the projects of the competitors, I continue my journey of knowledge of this great house, there is a splendid white room with a bright light , the transparent glass show a fabulous pool, there is a table that has a book that says instructions, important every day the meeting point will be at 7:45 on the ground floor of the building, which are in front of you at the center of all the houses, in fact it is easy to distinguish it, it is such a striking structure, its futuristic architecture stands out.

Well I think I'm going to rest, tomorrow we have a splendid day, I go to the sleeping area I imagine it must be like everything incredible, I climb the stairs and watch something great, it's a huge bed, this very large room has stay, a room, desk, the computer shows me on the monitor all the rooms in the house, oh great, I have a library of their own, they thought of everything, in all our needs, there is a function here, which tells me that it's an alarm clock, I'm going to program it at 6:50 in the morning, I'm going to have an excellent breakfast, I can schedule my breakfast, what I want and at what time I want it, I believe that breakfast at 7:05, until the computer It's great, it's on one side, almost reaching the door, embedded in the wall, as if it were part of it, it goes off alone and I can touch it on, yes, technology makes things easier for us, creates luxury anywhere or I would say it is a necessity.

I hear a heavenly voice, please get up is a new day, full of light and happiness, please get up today is a great day, a wonderful day, please get up, you will have a unique and special day, I get up, the alarm stops talk, digital disconnects, everything positive that I express, it's great because that little voice enters my subconscious, fills me with energy, I bathe and go down to the breakfast room, a juice of cranberries, apple and kiwi is served, it tastes great and the best which is fresh, cereal, whole wheat bread, yogurt, two bananas, an apple, a tomato juice and ready energy to start the day, I finish I relax I go to the bathroom and I go to the right place, the strength of knowledge.

The building where we will receive the classes, it is a great and fantastic sun, that gives energy to my whole body, we are gathered in the ground floor are 7:40 in the morning, 7:45 we are told to go up to some trolleys similar to the golf but modern, bigger, I read in the instructions that your fuel is the energy of the sun, what a wonder, they are fast are 7:50, we are in a great stadium, has an Olympic pool, there is a professional dives springboard , a race track, a building where there is a supergenial gym, the stadium is very futuristic, from what I read, it generates its own energy, this our Salomomr teacher with black sports lenses at the center of the stadium looks like a warrior ready to work , young competitors, I am impatient to start, impatient to know them, to study their mentality, their physical resistance, to know their personality, they are ready, we all answer if we are ready, I am going to give you a semblance of my I work, from now on there are no pretexts left abroad, in the past I can not, here in my class they will give their best effort, I will prepare them as some elite athletes, I know they are going to Hate at the beginning, but over time you will realize that the benefit and philosophy of life that you will get stuck in your heart, in your blood, in your thoughts, in your mentality, I want these words to come to your mind and then the heart is called;

The failure that became power

I tire of failure, I hate it with all my strength.

He introduced himself again, his impulse was such that it made me cry asking why?

The fear Increased, with the feeling of failing again.

My mind is upset, with the fear of continuing my way.

Failure is in my mind, I struggle day by day to disappear that terror.

I am full of rancor, shattered, desperate, I feel faint.

I am born again the light surrounds me, the energy is transported by my body.

The failure that became power, I feel it in my soul, in my spirit, in my heart.

All my courage, my rancor, my strength, they give death to failure.

I emerge again, I am reborn, with the mentality of being a winner.

Failure died, I am stronger, my experience helped me not to think about defeat.

I will give my whole body, all my energy, to be the best.

I am determined to leave a positive impression of my life.

So that my legacy is written in my mind and in the time that I always fight.

That I always made every effort to excel.

There was never a simple goal, every day was different, every day I delivered to the fullest.

My family, my loved ones, the population in general, knows that I am a warrior.

Failure became power, when I decided to be the best.

Failure became power, when I decided to fight until I died.

Failure became power, when I forget the pain, finding the experience.

Failure became power, when I knew that miracles exist.

The failure became power, when I met and the pretexts disappeared.

Failure became power, when I was born again.

I am your coach in this class there are no pretexts, all the exercises that you elaborate, I will also work on par with you, our group is one, we are one force, we are to support, understand and achieve success. We start what class my god, I hope to endure, we started doing physical exercise, then told us to run, we left the stadium through a tunnel climbed a mountain, we lowered it, we returned to the same place, we stretched, he sent us to the showers and told us, I see in the pool.

I am amazed everyone endured the exercises, I do not know if it was the philosophy that conveyed us in his words or that each competitor is an athlete, I say it was the philosophy, we are all hungry for success, if we are here it is because in our projects we have perseverance We swam a little over an hour, it was very tired, but we all endured the great elite training.

It's 10:15 the teacher tells us, today's competitors to finish the training, I was surprised their physical condition is splendid, they are great warriors, I thank them, the effort, the strength we demonstrate, let's join our hands and our war cry will be, we are champions and strong, so we shout It three times, stronger, come out of your heart, with strength, comrades, with strength, go for a sprinkler, have a great day, tomorrow see you , with the greatest strength.

How beautiful it is to exercise never had done this way, what a great teacher, I am surprised that I work just like us, all the routines, what a great teacher, what I have had only give you directions and you do everything, I loved this elite training is unique, the teacher looks very rough, but it is perfect that it is so, a disciplined and energetic group, is great, essential for development, and bañaditos and frescoes we go on the solar cars to the building, to to receive our next big class, we are on the ground floor at 10:50, they tell us to go up to the 19th floor that Professor Laeva is waiting for us with the Global Leadership subject.

We arrived at the big room at 10:55, well that everything is punctual and accurate that speaks very well of any organization, we begin at 11:00 a dynamic is performed where each of us introduce ourselves, along with the project and creation of each competitor, a brief explanation of the benefits that will be provided to the world population, what interesting projects, it is seen that they have been done with the soul, the heart, feelings and with great sensitivity, right now I have just heard all the projects are great, it's going to be very difficult for the judges, to choose the winner, but that's how the contests are. There are losers and only one winner, but my mentality says that all those who are here, by that simple fact, are winners, the Professor Laeva, competitors, it's great to listen to you, all the projects are spectacular, I consider all of you global leaders, they gave their hearts to each one of your projects, I feel proud to belong To this great group, now I will make my presentation talking to you with the following title;

Global leader

The world recognizes you, you have left a mark on several hearts.

You walk and turn back, you see countless followers.

You return to the past you relive your scars that were fresh.

It was not easy to obtain this great recognition.

During my journey there were too many failures, I got tired of so much failure.

The moment arrived when my mentality awoke with a supernatural force.

Stop fighting against the current and let me flow, it was a nice meeting.

My decision made me dream and believe in the greatest miracle, believe in me.

Believing in the synchronization of the universe, my act of faith grew.

On my loss path I met valuable people who joined me.

I built a great team, we became a single structure.

We started from scratch with the illusion that the great miracle would come.

After suffering, crying together, reflecting, the miracle that transformed us happened.

I became a global leader, who works with courage, feelings, sincerity and love.

My team accepted me, gave me the opportunity to lead, but I realized that we were still union and strength.

I am a global leader that depends on your team and the people around you.

I am a global leader, who struggles with the people around him to build.

I am a global leader, who believes in the projection of dreams.

I am a global leader, who believes in dreams.

I am a global leader, who believes in miracles.

I am a global leader, who believes in his people.

I am a global leader, who believes in the globalized world.

Competitors, you are a global leader, because you have thoughts towards the world population, the class is still too interesting, those words that the teacher just mentioned are great, any leader in the world, you should listen to them to come out with more courage, wishes to excel and make your team or organization reach development. Finish the great class, the interaction was great and to eat.

It's 12:45, in the instructions it said that the dining room is on the 26th floor, we are gathered in a beautiful dining room, we started to exchange words is great, we all set what we want to eat, I'm going to change some things is excellent have so much technology in the dining room, tactfully I mark my order again and at 12:55 we are all happy eating, it is beautiful to eat, the lounge music is great is instrumental, combined with jazz, rare instruments, but it relaxes me, we finish eating It's 13:40, we leave at 13:45 to the elevator, we play the next class on the 15th floor we arrive at the classroom at 13:55 our teacher is present, the class starts at 14:00, big competitors I am Teslac I will teach the Innovation class, I want everyone to present themselves, in conjunction with their project, I want them to be one person, go ahead, I want to know them, after everyone presented themselves in such an innovative way, each one expressed himself to the fullest , this concept helped the project to merge into a single idea, I am Teslac your teacher, all the projects you have presented are worthy of a prize, the premise that is observed is innovation, I love that the merger manifests itself, I introduce myself with this title;

Innovation

I felt no way out, no sense of real life.

I had a lot of people who depended on me, I thought, I watched, I thought again.

I could not find an exit, until the light illuminated me, an immense heat felt throughout my body.

I started to collect ideas, to listen, to look for alternatives, to dream.

Look at my exterior, strengthening my interior.

Collect the ideas, regroup my soldiers ready for business war.

The idea arose, our language was strengthened, innovation appeared.

A term easy to pronounce, difficult to apply.

Innovation, word officially added to our language.

Innovation, gave us teaching, learning and wisdom.

Innovation, gave us resources, personality, achievements, hopes.

Innovation, gave us creation, competence, patience, push.

Innovation, gave us freedom, awakened our dreams, synchronization, union.

Innovation, awakened our senses, taught us that we can make dreams come true.

Innovation, it taught us, that our personality grew, that it increased our social status.

Innovation, complement, structure, business base, alternative of global emergence.

Innovation, our minds went into action, they woke up from defeat and failure.

Innovation, gave us new proposals, made us invent, modernize our systems.

Innovation, gave us new ideas, which we project in new products.

Innovation, gave us a philosophy of service, to grow our procedures.

Innovation, gave us the opportunity to approach our clients in a spiritual way.

Innovation, in applying it, we knew the success and the process towards excellence.

Innovation, gave us a correct way to see the present, without imagining the greatness we will obtain in the future.

Innovation, a concept that changes societies by uniting the world.

Innovation, the factors of production are combined in a novel way.

Innovation, he told me that inventions are the key to economic growth.

Innovation, gave me a group of entrepreneurs, willing to fight until the end.

Innovation, gave me the interest and the search for new knowledge.

Innovation, gave me solutions and pleasure for the renovation.

Innovation, it taught me to create, to love, to unite, to visualize, to let myself flow.

Innovation, gave me a spiritual power a connection to the world.

Innovation, is creation, modernization, transformation, change.

Innovation, it's courage, love, hope, dreams, miracles fulfilled.

Innovation is a great value, power of decision, to be passionate.

Innovation is union and strength.

Competitors that is their life, that is their concept, that is why they must be willing to die, for the great word that is innovation. What a wonder my God, they are great the teachers speak with the heart, they reach the depths of our emotions, this is great, the emotions move everything, they give value and power, 15:45 the class ends, we go to the elevator we go to the floor 31, we are in the classroom are 15:55 the teacher is punctual in the room, hello to all, my best wishes, today we are about to start a great adventure, I am Professor McYuretzili, my subject is Communication and understanding, here in this moment the communications will be carried out in a deep way, working the body language to the fullest, using all the senses and emotions, here they will develop a real communication, I ask you please to each one of you, to tell me about your project Real way, that they sensitize their work, that they are transported to the spiritual sense of how their ideas came about, I want their project to express it to the fullest, I want them to communicate their ideas, to understand them and to know them In depth, if you want to be the best, you have to give the best, but with sensitivity, that reflect your ideas, your project, your feelings, we begin with the great adventure, they are the owners of the classroom.

Everyone communicated their project, there were tears, pain, spiritual sense, connection, what a great subject, it's great, in a class to learn to communicate in this way, I transform myself, I feel that joined the group more, those tears that occurred in this class, give us sensitivity, love our neighbor and be great observers of the sacrifice that was made before we got here, there were failures that gave us more strength, understanding, love, hope, it's 17:45 the beautiful class ends, we're headed again to the elevator, to room 22 we start at 18:00, the next class, the teacher's voice is heard, competitors are welcome, I am his teacher Edisonic, the subject that I will teach is Transcendental Ideas, which I explain to you with this, that ideas have been the object of veneration, shared at all times, often kept as valuable treasures, on countless occasions they were not shared, but what we know throughout history and that there have been countless ideas but there are few that transcend or live forever, I want each of you to present yourself with your name, to manifest an idea of the past that is present, with its respective author, ahead competitors I hear them, all begin to express themselves, some ideas are well known, but others have been forgotten, but the great thing about this is that the exchange of ideas enriches us, gives us more learning, gives us a unique analysis.

Good competitors very grateful, for their exchange of information, they did this enriching class, it is short the time that we interact, but we have learned something important, that many times, it requires a lot of time, I thank you for your great contribution that you have an excellent night. We finished precisely at 18:55, we went to the 23rd floor, we entered it is an excellent aroma, a soft music that penetrates the ears like a celestial whisper.

The teacher comes out completely dressed in white, speaks with a piercing voice hello competitors welcome to this energy field here they will fill their energy bodies, to rest in peace, so that the new day ideas flow, increase learning, experience and arrive the precious treasure that is the wisdom I am your teacher Noetherli, Yoga Bioenergetics, is the energy that will reach all your bodies, the aura of the universe will teach you to receive with abundance, everything that life provides, every detail no matter how minimal fill them in the consciousness of our ancestors, ready to start, the teacher shows us many yoga positions that we are performing at your own pace, it is a delight to receive this great class is 7:00 p.m.

Guys we are finished, this is how your deep breathing must be, the air that you breathe is yours, accept what nature gives you, receive everything with abundance, enjoy it, enjoy, use all your senses, we own the most valuable things in the world that is our body, we are millionaires have infinite wealth, we have eyes, that has no technological machine in the world, our whole body is a powerful machine, great, unique, appreciate your body, is an incomparable treasure, use magic of your body, all the senses must work, your sensory capacity must be attentive to the outside and inside of you, fill yourself with energy, take advantage of your energy to realize positive capacities, join positivism, complement your life with creative ideas, I your teacher Noetherli, I wish you a pleasant night, in what you create, please reflect your gratitude, ask for strength, to continue your journey with magic and lots of energy, smile, enjoy this great moment, because it is unique, special, wonderful, fantastic, great and incomparable.

Enjoy life to the fullest, enjoy every moment as if it were the last in their lives, that will teach them to live to the fullest, with dedication, strength, coordination, spirituality and love. What a great day, full of much learning, dreams, hopes, miracles, I wonder, if education was this way, students would go to school happy, with enthusiasm, wanting to learn something new, the dynamics that They showed in the classes are great, they are worthy of recognition and imitation, in fact if the classes were like this they would increase the knowledge, the education would be excellent, the competences would be great in the societies, if a culture of development in the education was created, the societies would improve, the quality of life would be productive, the systems would have better trained personnel, would be fought for a mutual benefit and at the same time generalized, it would be great, pleasant, to attend school, with these teachings and ways of working, it would increase the exchange of ideas, countless projects would be carried out for the benefit of the societies, the population in general would enjoy a satisfactory social status I will fulfill all your needs, well I will go to my great home, oh suddenly I see that someone climbs the mountain, goes to the Taoci spiritual guru, I can not distinguish it, I hurry to my house to check the images of the temple , I start to review the images of monitor A1.

CHAPTER III

I am observing the competitor does not appear, who will be, what he wants, it is the first day of classes and they are already resorting to the Guru, it must be something important, just enter not reach it to distinguish, I will make the approach is Mahatmae from India, good evening Guru Taoci, I am, the Guru's voice is heard, stop and say no more, I know what Mahatmae has come for, but I want you to speak with sincerity and heart, to help you and give you an answer to enlighten you spiritually, guru I am sad and worried, the classes were great, but I am very exhausted, wanting to give up and go to India, I feel that maybe my project will not be effective, son the mind often creates chaos and nonexistent conflicts, that maybe will not even happen, but I understand you, you are not used to this kind of classes, to this type of knowledge, but really, you will realize with the passing of days, that this knowledge they transmit the Teachers is unique, because you are free to be creative and innovative, respect your beliefs, but you must be more spiritual, be grateful for the small details, ask fervently for the achievement of your goals and objectives, fight daily as much as possible. Last day you are in this place, let yourself go, flow like water do not stop, but with strength and determination.

The changes are difficult, necessary to improve, come closer to me, sit face to face, the guru places his hand on the surface of the head while listening to a mantra that comes from within, at the end he listens to the son I have revised in a spiritual way your life, I have penetrated, through the stormy abysses that you have gone through and I have observed some lights that have always been with you, you have had a difficult life, you have suffered, you have cried, you have asked yourself the Why? Of your sufferings, you have sought explanations, you have asked your God, because all this happens to you, I understand you when reviewing your life, but I say something to you since we are born, we never imagined the future that we are going to have, you have I suffered too much because your father was an alcoholic, he treated your mother badly, brothers and you, he even tried to kill you several times, if your child cries you have to leave all that pain, count on me, I will help you to follow your spiritual path, you have spent a lot suffering, in my mind is your life story, I will not tell you all because you already know it, what I will be that you realize, that many times the situations that happen are for something, a form of knowledge that you have not understood yet.

I know it is difficult, because of the heavy burden of suffering that you carry, I recognize that you are a great person, that vices have avoided you to the fullest, that during your life journey, you have sought positive personalities, positive images, you have struggled to maintain a light in your path, that has benefited you a lot, imagine, begin to reflect, in the great place that you are, with the great responsibility to contribute with your ideas and knowledge for the Mission, eliminate world poverty, I'll tell you something I want you to keep in your heart and when you feel lost, you have no hope, solution, open your heart for these words to come out, it is hard to tell you, incomprehensible, but it is reality, suffering is necessary in our lives, it hurts very much , makes us faint, but suffering gives us personality, gives us the guts to face whatever comes our way, imagine that you would have had an exemplary life, the one you would have wished, would not be a gu errero

A warrior is born when there are battles, during your life you have had many battles, they have given you a positive perspective of what the world is, if you had not suffered you would not have fighting spirit, that energy that you show in storms, always let yourself flow, God is witness to what is happening to you, but yes, you must fight forever to never give up, every day observe it as a different day, where your strength will resurface, you will end exhausted, you will rest and wait for the new day, I have noticed in you something important that someday I will tell you, in your mind keep your tools for the war of life, persevere, bold, determined, consent, when you least expect it, the treasure so precious that is the wisdom , look for it forever, forget about the material that comes alone, locate yourself in obtaining the most precious treasure that is wisdom, how do you feel? Guru, great sir, I feel fantastic, with an inexplicable energy, I am ready to face whatever comes my way, I love those words, I like your power of decision, your Mahatmae, you have the solution to all your problems.

When you realize what surrounds you and internalize your abilities, your way of thinking is enriched, when you speak with sincerity and from the heart, the solutions arrive, my son go with God, rest relax, strengthen your energies because tomorrow awaits you a great job, hug the guru, it looks like a child hugging his father, there is God this learning is great, as a psychologist, I feel that I still need to learn, every day is different, unique and special, experiences that You get reflected in the knowledge that you transmit, I am amazed as the guru knew who visited him, as he knows all his life, that my god, I thought that only existed in fiction films, what a great day, my God, is a great day the first day, what day wealth, well I'm going to have dinner, I go to the library for a book and to sleep.

The alarm sounds are 6:50, it was very short the night, after breakfast and bath, I'm ready, we're all together at 7:40, we take the cars that their fuel is solar energy, if they should be all the cars, in fact the environment would improve, we would have the ability to have a fresh, pure air, global warming would disappear from our language, we would have a world with the ideal conditions of life, they are 7:50 Professor Salomomr is as always , in the center of the stadium, sports clothes with lenses, has a warrior personality, his voice is strong, clear, welcome to a new day competitors, as you know today is the class Sports Philosophy and Training we started with philosophy;

Life philosophy

How many times have you wished you were not in a place, not confronting yourself, not fighting.

But life is full of challenges, difficulties, failures, losses.

But life goes on, if you want to be a winner, you must be willing to suffer.

After the storms, when calm comes, it's time to build.

Your life is full of challenges, that is to live.

You are not the owner of the past and the future, you are the owner of this moment.

Your tears have remained in the past.

But your scars will never disappear, your tears will return.

Better live the present to the fullest, you are the owner of this great moment.

If you have to enjoy do it to the fullest, if you have to fight, fight hard.

You have hate, courage, transmit all that energy and convert it into positive energy.

You are the master of your thoughts, you have a great machine that is your body.

Work day by day, without waiting for the results, when you least expect it, knock at your door the big surprise.

What you sow is what you will reap, if you sow initiative, perseverance, fervor, love, wealth will surround you.

Wealth is not only material, it is spiritual.

You must be a great observer of the small details, you must enjoy those gifts.

Do not be afraid, be careful.

Do not have a grudge, the negative change it for love.

Fight to the maximum, so that future generations, observe your footprint and follow it.

Laugh, enjoy, be responsible, punctual, have an ethic that projects your personality.

The philosophy of life is in you, it belongs to you, you complete those chapters that will distinguish you.

The philosophy of life complements your parameters of existence.

The philosophy of life, is your life story with spirituality and love.

The philosophy of life is a complement to your existence in this world.

The philosophy of life, is how you face the storms, the challenges, yourself.

The philosophy of life, is energy, cause, effect, is love.

Competitors I know that things in life are not easy, but if we analyze, we evaluate, we have to realize that everything has its degree of difficulty, I want each of you to tell me that you thought yesterday's training and what meaning it gives you to his life.

Each of the competitors spoke with great philosophy, a special sense, but when I touch Florencet said, Professor I analyze part of the night and my question is, what is this for? I am a gymnast, part of my life I have done a lot of exercise, I feel that we come to this place to develop our project, not to be elite athletes, thanks Florencet, for your interesting question, who believe that since yesterday I was waiting this big question, in reality physical exercise is for many things, but I mention them in a limited but clear way; it is so that they do not get sick, increase their mental health, reduce stress, disappear fear, that their blood sugar levels are good, control their weight, increase learning capacity, concentration, alertness, so they have a pleasant quality of sleep, having a restful and deep sleep, strength in all your muscles, strengthening your heart, having an athletic personality, I can spend all day talking about the benefits, but this is in summary, I am clear, all answered yes, well if there are no doubts to work we started.

As we finished the big task, after swimming we bathed and headed to the building is 10:50, we go to the 32nd floor are 10:55 we are in the classroom our teacher observes us, patient, welcome competitors I am Mark I them I will teach the subject Human Development, you are leaders must handle profiles of effective imitation, I mean with this, that there are countless people who imitate them, at the end of this project they are all winners, everyone will turn them to see and observe all Your accomplishments, your behaviors, your ethics, your positive and negative implements, I want each of you to present yourself in a random way, with the premise, to tell me 5 things that identify you as positive people, I listen to you later, after Everyone expressed himself, I think it's a great presentation, competitors thank you very much for your feedback, it's great to hear them, now I introduce myself with the following title;

Human development

I've worried forever, for me.

I have lived in a bubble where I am the only one who lives there.

I've forgotten others, I know I can help them, but I've avoided them.

I want to get out of the bubble, but the pretexts prevent me from leaving.

I like to love myself, to think only of myself, because I will think of others.

In this bubble I am excellent, I feel special, I do not lack anything.

But I realize that I'm missing something great, which is to convey what I know.

I'm afraid to get out of the bubble, I've lived there a long time, I got used to it.

But today is a new day, I decide to change to worry about others.

Anyone would say that I do not gain anything, but the experience I receive is the path to self-realization.

I was scared, I destroyed the bubble, but there were times I imagined being in it.

Until social relations gave me the opportunity to be another.

I gave everything I had without expecting to receive something in return.

I develop a great word that until today I use it as a premise.

Human development, it's my job, it's my life, it's my dedication.

It is a difficult job, but one that enriches me and leads me to the great path of wisdom.

Knowing many people, gives me the joy of knowing infinite behaviors.

The experience makes human development my priority in this life.

Human development circulates through my blood, I am happy to belong to you.

I have my legacy, for whom to live for Human Development.

I feel that my life makes sense, because I have shaped everything, in human development.

Human development a word, that has a lot of wealth, a lot of spirituality, many minds, many reasons.

Human development I am willing to give my life, my soul and my spirit.

Human development, development of life, development of the world.

I am your teacher Markl, willing to take you through the great adventure of human development, what great words, what presentation, 12:45 ends the class, now if we eat, we go to the large dining room, everyone looks enthusiastic, jovial, with much energy, which is why Professor Salomomr has it, in fact exercise is a source of life, it gives you a lot of energy, vision, joy, everyone feels fresh, joyful and happy conversations flow, enjoying the sacred foods, we finish eating To the sanitary, we wash our mouths, what freshness now if ready for the next class.

It's 13:55 we're in the classroom, our teacher is watching us, hello, good young people, let's start, I'm his teacher Vincir, I have the privilege of teaching the subject that moves the world, the subject of the great of all time, Creativity, which great word, I want each of you to present your project, but with the creative idea that was manifested at that moment, after listening to all the great projects as they came up, the teacher observed them carefully, he says great, I like how he started that Great project with the biggest manifestation that is creativity.

Throughout our history there have been creative minds that have emerged from nothing, even countless creators, were not excellent in school, or labeled with an illness, it was difficult for them to resurface from all that negativity, it happens very often When we feel that all the doors are closed, we can not find an exit, the only key that is considered of us is creativity, everything starts with a dream, an idea, until it becomes reality, society, the people that surround us or even relatives often do not believe in us, it is important to always demonstrate with facts, that dreams can come true, if our great inventors of all times, had not acted in the face of adversity, we would not enjoy their great creations, they all had the courage to face all the negative facts that were presented to them and they never gave up, we must thank their great courage, to present their ideas, in the course of our history even some creative beings died for their ideals, before the ignorance that at that time did not understand the value they were providing to humanity, all their creations are an advance for the population of the whole world, the Technology, together with creativity, creates modernization, values, time reduction, efficiency, coordination, production, profits, development, history shows us that creativity has been present at all times, creative ideas have been construction, all inventions that we observed around us, started with an idea, that's how his great project began, steps are needed to finish it, but what I do tell you is to fight for your ideas, when you believe in something that can produce benefits, do not hesitate to fight for its realization, I know that you will encounter obstacles of all kinds, but in the end you have the decision, that if you want to make your dream come true.

Creativity in any project is the most important, to be accepted worldwide, your product must be innovative, meet the needs of the population, you who have the mission, eliminate world poverty, is such a big responsibility, but at the same time, it is something unique and new, never in all history, in all times, has a project as important as this been done, that the priority is to benefit the population of the world, which suffers from this great problem. under his shoulders a heavy burden, but I have good news, when I heard each of his projects, I did not know which would be the winner, because they were all made with the premise of solving the big problem in the world, congratulations are all winners, for the judges within almost a month, it will be difficult for them to choose the competitor who will leave. Competitors invite you to merge, join, complement each other, with the great concept that is creativity, you already know this word they applied it in their projects, each class will know better the creativity, we will study the great creators, only We will take a synthesis of each one of them, it will be an analysis, of their most important ideas, that will benefit our lives, that all these authors will transmit to us their philosophy, their wisdom, their history of life, that in our way we have part of Their tools that immortalized them, their capacity for perseverance, their self-efficacy, their self-control, will be a priority for us.

The class continued, the teacher showed us a great path that creative beings have left in this world, that magnificent class ends at 15:45, we go to the elevator floor 24, it is 15:55 the teacher observes us, hello competitors, I hope you are amazed in this place, because you already know that it belongs to you, I want you to present each one of you, I want to add to your presentation 5 words that motivate you, we started guys, each one was observed with a special joy when they said what I motivated them, since the teacher listened to everyone said great guys, I love their words, I think all they mentioned are necessary, interesting, that in times of crisis make you resurface, competitors I am Professor Curielm, I give them again welcome your motivation, my presentation is as follows;

The motivation

It lights my whole body, with a special energy that does not burn me, but that strengthens me.

He taught me that life is beautiful, I have a sense of strength to live immensity.

I fill my heart with hope, with vitality, with weapons to fight.

I learned that dreams come true, that ideas are transformed.

That the impulse of creation motivated me to action.

Optimism knocked on my door, taught me that there is a solution.

I wrote my goals and objectives, I am carrying them out, step by step.

Time is not an impediment, but every day I try my best.

My knowledge and learning, are a muscle that I exercise daily.

I motivate those around me by valuing their self-esteem and confidence.

Body language gives me energy teaches me that synchronization is strength.

I surround myself with positive people, who motivate me to follow my path.

I have mistakes and failures that motivate me to fight harder.

I feel that my achievements and my strengths teach me that with work and discipline everything is reborn.

The motivation, is my partner.

Motivation has seen me cry, suffer, laugh, I carry the motivation in my blood.

Motivation taught me that achievement behaviors are acquired responsibly.

Motivation taught me that love is the structural basis of any project.

Motivation is my soul, my spirit, my religion.

Motivation is a treasure that gives meaning to my life.

The motivation, has given me the courage, the courage to continue on my way fighting decisively.

The motivation understood me in times of crisis, it gave me perseverance.

Motivation is all that I need to achieve my goals and objectives.

Motivation, motivation is part of my body, it is a necessity.

The motivation in the weather was my sun.

I am a warrior full of motivation and happiness.

Competitors I invite you to use, this tool necessary for the proper functioning of individuals, groups and the population in general, you have to be great motivators, in our classes you will find the bases of the most successful men and women in the world, you will find your life stories, they will know that success is not very far from you, they have to look for it with need, motivation, discipline, they have to motivate the world with their projects. What great classes, my God, with which learning I will retire from here, everything I am seeing is worthy of several doctorates, they are knowledge, structured, of magnificent experiences, by taking out the wealth of knowledge, the time is very fast, it is over the teacher's great class, it is 17:45, we go to the elevator to the 10th floor, we arrive another special class awaits us, I feel great motivation, we are all in the classroom the teacher tells us that we are in a , all the furniture we make an u, the teacher is in the center of the u, sitting in a university type chair with a little more modernity.

Hi, I'm all teacher Yessica, I'm going to teach the Positive Mentality subject, all of you have a positive mentality, I want everyone to tell me 3 things, that made them get the mentality they have, first they tell me their name, we start Right to left, as they finished, the teacher says, it's great to listen to them, I thank them all for their sincerity, all this feedback gives me more knowledge about you, this positive mentality that belongs to them, unconsciously everyone is attached to their mentality, what they I want to imply, that the magic of this mentality is that it goes with you to any place, is in any challenge, tomorrow in the training class, they will realize what I tell them, what I do not like is As it runs fast the time is 18:55,

I thank you for your great comments, the class is over, have a good rest for tomorrow.

We retired from the fabulous class was very short, I spend very fast time, we go to the 23rd floor, Professor Noetherli is in front of us in lotus flower position, she tells us welcome students please stand in front of me in the same position that I represent, the lotus flower in yoga, breathe deeply close your eyes, transport your mind projecting something that is to your liking, continue to breathe, feel as the air is transported throughout your body, feel that energy, flowing through your Inside, you hear music that I feel in my stomach, students open their eyes, extend their hands, absorb all the energy that surrounds them, we begin, we perform energetic yoga positions, we finish the delight of the positions, please return to occupy the same position with which you started, listen to the beat of your heart, close your eyes again, today this class is the knowledge of finding yourself, here in the present, in this instantly, we are owners of this great moment, my spiritual sense is reborn, my soul is transported, my life is beautified, it is filled with light, I feel the heat that runs through my veins, it ignites my body with energy, my fears have disappeared, my energetic aura emerges, the darkness disappears, I find myself in a place that breathes tranquility, I feel floating, I am a spirit, in a wonderful place, my initiative grows, my sense of life is strengthened, the love flows through my heart, I love my body, everything that surrounds me, there is a white color of purity, which manifests freedom.

I see my loved ones, I give them a hug, I tell them how happy I feel to see them, that they are part of me, that the work I am doing is for the benefit of my loved ones and the world population, my legacy will ignite infinity of hearts, will be combined with the spirit and the soul, the universe is a witness of my sincere intentions, of my struggle, of my suffering, I remain in the past, today in this day I am victorious, this moment is mine, I feel happy, my legacy is going to be fantastic wonderful, only God knows my conscience, only God is the owner of life, God is a witness of my vocation, who is enveloped by love, please open your eyes slowly, I see tears in some eyes, feel happy, your heart has expressed its sincerity, feel the relief of your whole body, we have finished for this day, this great day that saw us bloom, gave us the universe the opportunity, to meet with the soul and with the magnificent spiritual side, that ignited East place, which ignited our hearts, we end today but our souls are still in the world, crossing the immensities, crossing the uncertainty, sensitizing themselves to what surrounds them, have a good night, it is 20:00.

What a fabulous and spiritual class, I'm going to my house, I'm going to observe, I think no one will go up to see the spiritual Guru, as if someone would come up, there is a bell that warns me, I'm going to rest, what a wonderful day , in each class, there is a lot of wisdom, it is a special learning, never seen, it would be envy of any institution or rather it would be worthy to imitate, there is a home, a magnificent and sweet home, I think now if I go to have a relaxed dinner, when I was for my dinner, the doorbell rang, who will be the one who turns to the Guru, I can not see who he is, he is already in the temple of the guru, I am going to zoom in on the lens, and to the location.

Hello Mr. Guru Taoci, hi daughter was thinking about you, I know what you are coming to, you are Joharim from South Africa, I know you have had a difficult life, but I hear you speak to me with my heart, I want you to know that you have me, is that today In the last class we just had, some thoughts that torment me, it hurts me to return to that past of great pain, Professor Noetherli, transported us to the past and I felt as if something had pierced my heart, it was a huge pain, I'm sorry as if this moment is happening, if your daughter is not afraid to express your feelings, cry, return to that stormy past, do not avoid it, you have to face it, say what you feel.

I feel a huge grudge because life has treated me this way, when I was almost 3 years old my mom died in a plane crash, it was a pain that does not go away, I've had it all my life, in school when moms attended a festival, I was alone as a dog, my teachers some understood my pain, I have always asked Why? I did not have a breast, I have received many answers during my life, but no one replaces my mother, that is my greatest desire in my life, do not expect riches, my only desire to know my mom, live with her, love her, ask her for advice, leave with her, I feel that my life has no meaning, I am very depressed, I feel defeated, I understand you daughter is very difficult, there are losses, but that of a being so close, is normal what you feel, I congratulate you, because although you do not appreciate it, you have come very far despite your pain, your great obstacle, the lack of your mother, the grief that you live on a daily basis, is a wound that will always be open, that pain you feel you should not avoid , you must let it flow, feel the pain, cry, the moment will come when you least expect it, the suffering will diminish as if by magic, the great miracle will come, you will imagine that your mother is in all beautiful things, that is proud of you, that even if you do not see it, you will feel A smile, an immense happiness, you will never forget your mother, but the pain will diminish, you will meet other people, you will have other activities, you will have a family to fight for, you will realize that love is immense, that it is universal, you will become more spiritual, you will enjoy forever what we call small details, which are spiritual riches.

You must fight as you have always done, with perseverance, dedication, passion and love, you know that your mom watches you, wherever you are, the goals, goals you project, whether they are short, medium or long term, are going to be significant in your life, you know that you will transcend, that your legacy that you are making, will be a creation of ideas and dreams, that when you least expect it will come true, life does not end in the past, life is in the present, the future is uncertain, you are the owner of this great moment, you have to live and enjoy life to the fullest, as if you were about to die, that will make you enjoy every moment, not having a sense of time, you only live to the fullest with what is yours this instant, the present, close your eyes come closer, dream at this moment visualize your mother, for a few moments, do not tell me anything until I tell you to open your eyes, also open the eyes of your soul, feel a warmth that run for your body, smile, you're with your mom, tell mummy, tell her everything you want, this moment is yours, slowly open your eyes, wipe away tears, wake up alive, I want you to tell me what was your experience, that you speak to me with you soul and you heart.

I told him cute mommy because you left, because you left me so lonely, I did not deserve you to leave, I really need you, my daughter there are things, situations in life that you can not predict, only God knows the threads of our destiny, I I did not want to die and leave you alone, it has also been an immense pain, my only resignation and happiness is knowing that you are well, that you are a great warrior, that you fight with a lot of perseverance for what you want, that you are very intelligent, disciplined, responsible, I can continue talking a lot of concepts that you already know, here in this place I am, it is a spiritual place, full of light, I can see you, when you suffer, I suffer, when you laugh, I laugh, if you are happy, I I am also, I am a reflection of what your life is, then what I want from you daughter, my love, my hope, my life, what I desire with fervor is that you be happy, daughter everyone in the world is going to die, some before, others after, but it is the law of life all mor They will go in the world, that's why I invite you daughter to value your life to the fullest, take her as a beautiful and precious treasure, take care of her, be happy.

 Do not worry so much about problems, be optimistic about life, I'm not physically with you, but always keep in mind that my spirit is at your side and observe what happens to you, I am your mirror of your behaviors, my daughter fight always for happiness, joy, love, select the important things in your life, give them priority, be brave to enjoy what life gives you, be grateful for what you receive no matter how small, my daughter as well as you, I take you in my heart, I am very proud of you, when you need me I will be with you in a spiritual way, I will take care of you, but do not look for negative situations, turn your mind completely positive, the attraction towards fantastic and wonderful things, it will be a magnet that you will have to attract the best things in life, dream my daughter, because miracles exist, I congratulate you, you are a great woman, I am proud of you forever.

My daughter show the world because you are here, in this life, fight to be the best, leaving a trace of your interventions, socializing, contributing to a better world, I say goodbye to my love, from today I want you to be clear that I am with you, in good and bad, you are my beloved daughter, I love you, do not leave me mom, hug me, thanks mom, I love you too and thank you because I know you are by my side, thanks for talking with me, you know how much I need you, I say goodbye and you will always be proud of your daughter Joharim, guru that was what I talked with my mom, you realize how wonderful the universe is, what you needed is to have a spiritual contact with your mom, I congratulate you daughter, for that great encounter, in this life daughter there is much pain, many duels, but you know what is important and wonderful, to take the beautiful, fantastic, beautiful, that gives us life, when you give love, you receive much love, remember daughter that what sow, it is what you will harvest, your life is fruitful, you are a wonderful woman, ready to fight, that characterizes you.

Daughter ask God our Lord, that you strength or what you believe, even the universe is witness to your great spirituality, daughter feel happy, rest tonight recover your energy, because tomorrow is a new day, let me hug you great guru , thank you for your advice, thanks for your support, thank you for listening to me, daughter, count on me forever, I am here to help you, thank you for your trust daughter, this wonderful temple is your home.

Out Joharim, what a great experience it was to observe all this, it was such a feeling that I also cry, I realize that emotions are contagious, I do not strongly agree observing in this monitor, all that reliability, but that's right, this study, my ethics is ready for all this great project, it is magnificent to be sensitized with what happens to other people, our real personalities often hide our problems, but each person has a great life story, we are unique, only we know the emotional load that we carry on our shoulders, good to sleep because tomorrow awaits me a great day.

It is 7:55 we are in the center of the stadium, hello guys yesterday were in my class, as you know I am the teacher Yessica the subject that I will teach is called; Training special forces, I want you to listen before we start training this title philosophy;

Today

I have left the chains that stopped me, that had me imprisoned.

It's a new day, the past has disappeared, I'm living in the present.

The triumphs that gave me pleasure have disappeared, it's a new day.

The failures that made me tremble have disappeared, it is a new day.

I will deliver to the fullest, in my goals and objectives.

I will make 1 effort 2, 3, 4,5 ... whatever is necessary.

I will laugh, I will enjoy, I will fight, I will enjoy, it is a new day.

I will sensitize myself, with the people around me.

I will be more spiritual, I will look at the fantastic and wonderful things that surround me.

I have a lot of energy, I am willing to die fighting, persevering.

I am a warrior, willing to demonstrate his courage, building.

I own this moment, this moment is mine, I will do the best.

I have the responsibility to transcend, I will do my best role in this world.

I dream of a better world, I dream of a spiritual world, of a world with love.

I give myself body and soul to my activities.

I surround myself with positive people, who have the same objective to build.

The storms disappeared, the sun was born.

I am a new individual determined to succeed, determined to pay the price.

I am capable of risking everything, for a better world.

Today is important is time to transcend.

Today is the time to make ideas and dreams come true.

Today is the time to work with enthusiasm, strength, dedication.

Today is the time to write the history of life that will leave its mark.

Today is the time to make the most effort, finding the expected results.

Today is the time to live, with the mentality of a champion.

Today is the time to build the seed that will give the expected results.

Today the world will hear my voice, the prayers will sound in my mind and in my heart.

Today I am willing to give my life.

Today my spirit and my soul will travel the universe.

Today I am determined to transcend.

Today, today, simply and only today ...

You guys have the decision, the rules are manifested, the capabilities are created, the strength, discipline, perseverance is built, the pretexts are eliminated from our vocabulary, we start with the training of special forces, we start with great enthusiasm, but suddenly in physical exercise, fell Jenst, all surprised we surrounded him asking if he was okay, I twisted my ankle, the teacher reviews it, you want me to talk to medical services, I do not feel good, that believes that in my sport Rugby, I am accustomed to stronger injuries, you can continue, if I can continue, continue the fabulous exercise, we stay in the pool and finish the great class, showed us Professor Yessica, who has a surprising condition, with her in charge they finished the pretexts.

The classes continued with the fabulous philosophy, which gives us wisdom and transports us to the world of knowledge, which all these professors transmit, the classes are so sophisticated, that they focus on each of the presented projects, every detail, every experience, gives a more real perspective of life, gives us global leadership, that focuses on the needs of the population, each class is a great construction for each of the towers that were created, in each class they are polished for a better presentation and elaboration of the objectives and goals, we finish the classes for today, I retire to my house, what a great day, I realize that each day is different, that each day gives you a gift, a new learning, the experience grows, the needs of each day, make us more creative.

I am in my house, the doorbell rings again, who will go to visit the guru Taoci, I watch him on the monitor, it is Jenst, I imagine it is because of his injury in the training of special forces, of the teacher Yessica. Says guru Taoci, son explain to me that you come out words with feeling and your heart, guru I am depressed I have had during my sport Rugby, infinity of injuries but I feel that this twist is affecting me more than anything, I feel a burden heavy that does not let me continue and this great pain that I feel unbearable, approach son show me your injury, come closer, the guru closes his eyes he keeps meditating, mentioning a mantra that comes from his insides he says uuuuuummmmm, penetrates his voice in the whole temple, Touch with the left hand the ankle injury, a bright light appears, that light is disappearing it looks as if it will be inserted, in the Jenst's injury.

Son you can open your eyes, how you feel, oh my God, it's a miracle, the pain disappeared, I can jump and run as if nothing had happened, I feel happy guru, if your son is in connection with your soul and spirit, it's the most beautiful thing that can exist, I hear you son, guru I felt finished, defeated, wanting to be the first to retire, I felt that my self-esteem deteriorated since I arrived here, I feel that this project is too much for me, when I was 11 years something terrible happened in my life my parents separated, I felt that my world was ending, my dad used drugs, when he did not do it he treated me very well, but when he resorted to drugs, he humiliated me, he said that it was useless, It was trash, I beat my mom, I suffered a lot, I have no brothers, no family, all I had was my parents, I wanted to disappear, I wanted to die, but I was stopped by the only love I have received in my life, my mother's, I stayed with her, my father disappeared, I never knew more about him, it was very hard in my life, I have always looked for ideal parents, it has worked for me, because those that I have found have helped me to form, they have transmitted wisdom, some advice has helped me in times of storms, I always cried at night asking God because I did not have a good father, with whom I could play, laugh, talk, admire him and wish to be like him, my mom, I played the two roles of father, mother At the time, it helped me a lot to grow and mature, it gave me the love I needed, the support, a lot of love, if the child cries, get out of bed, it is healthy to cry, more when the pain comes from deep inside the heart.

If you have had a complicated life and I admire your determination as you have developed, in the great pain that enveloped you during your growth, but my son, when you have an exemplary life, without pain, without problems, it is when you do not appreciate what you have , you have to live a complicated life, it is hard to say, but all this suffering has shaped you, has given you wisdom and sometimes immunity to pain, often considered harmful pain, but if you analyze the events that have caused you formed during the past, has been experience, that has given you courage, decision, has taught you to appreciate the things that we often call simple and that are the most valuable, your character has been formed, your perseverance, your dedication, some of your fears have disappeared, but the human being has never just learned, every day is a new day of teachings, every day you must fight to surrender to the maximum in your activities, in this life nothing is easy, everything has its degree of difficulty, the important thing is the experience you get, it helps you to defend yourself against the adversities of life, we must accept and receive the life that was given to us, in the best way, to live each day enjoying the best of life, struggling with courage and determination, before the obstacles that arise, my son appreciates what you have, you have come very far and your path is still very long.

If you maintain a true enthusiasm, you must prepare yourself for the infinity of riches that you are about to receive, the theme of your project to build happiness, it is a very difficult job that awaits you, but you must motivate yourself, show enthusiasm, be happy, be willing until doing the impossible so that your project has the expected success, your mind must be open to feedback, the classes you receive are a good complement to your development, your mom is proud of you, someday you will have a family, with the one that you are going to live with, demonstrate your leadership, your love, your spirituality, always give the best of you, that your impulses come from the soul and the heart, complement yourself socializing with positive people, that coincide in your ideas and projects, be happy, Feel proud because you are a builder of happiness, for the world population, on your shoulders is a heavy burden, that with time you will get used to carrying, you like challenges and life is full of challenges, my son pray to God who gives you strength and the most important thing is wisdom, thank you very much guru Taoci, I have received your advice as a father to a helpless son, thanks you have made me understand in this short time, my sense of life, because I am in this world, my mother will feel happy and proud of her son forever, thanks guru, for healing me physically and mentally, I take you in my mind and my heart great teacher, son rests renews your energies, that tomorrow a great day awaits you.

I watch Jents, he can walk well, his body language is different from what I present when he arrived with the guru, I see him more determined, he breathes better, his self-esteem went up, his senses are awake, his mentality is alert, what is great to hear to the guru, I am surprised how he knows the history of people before they tell him he already knows what they are coming from, his philosophy is enriching, his healing is dazzling, magical, heals physically, mentally, emotionally, each life story is amazing, the learning that is obtained is fabulous, the knowledge of different personalities gives us enrichment, that I work so fabulous to find myself in this place full of knowledge, I go out of my house, deep breath enters through my body clean air, fresh air, that recharges me of energy, I see the sky I observe the magnificent stars, the greatness of the universe, as we are insignificant before the greatness that surrounds us, the view is fantastic, as we It makes perceive, great situations, unique moments, pleasant experiences, great day my god, it is a dream come true, belong to a great project, this is great, never in my mind I happen to belong to something significant, that is of benefit to the world population, which is one of the most significant projects in the history of mankind, good to rest that tomorrow awaits us a great day full of learning, wisdom, unique and wonderful experiences.

What a fabulous day it's Friday, it's been a great week, it's 18:55, it's about to begin, our great Bioenergetic Yoga class, with Professor Noetherli, young people in their hands have a mantra, all in the lotus position, their breaths have to be deep, with your eyes closed, only with awareness awake, breathe deeply see the light that surrounds you, is a light, that energizes your bodies, open your eyes, the sheet you hold in your hands has words that go to repeat deeply, inhale and exhale, the word comes out crucial, the word should come out of your energy center;

OM

LAM

VAM

RAM

YAM

I'M HAPPY

I'M STRONG

THE LIFE IS LOVE

GOD IS ALL

It is repeated again

Get up please tell me what your feelings were, each one showed the enthusiasm that karma produced, says the teacher, I am glad that the objective of this class has been achieved, that each of you had a spiritual reunion, get out of our world by means of a great mantra is something wonderful, there comes a time when your body is the one speaking, the transmissions of relief that it expresses, you see in your attitude, even though your days have been exhausting of great effort, this mantra has awakened them enthusiastically, with the complement of the union of the being with the universe, you can read the mantra when you need, find yourself, your spirituality enhances your life on earth, love our body and keep it in communication with the senses is necessary for mental, emotional and spiritual development, I finish this great day take the class in your mind and your heart, rest, may God bless you with fruitful lives and full.

What a beautiful class, that mantra makes a great connection, I felt so spiritual that at those moments, I forgot where I was, as the teacher said, I believe that I travel to a special place in the universe, I go to my house, it was a unique day, to dine and to sleep, tomorrow awaits us one day as all special, awake is Saturday, we have the great training exploration special forces, by Professor Salomomr and Professor Yessica, together I imagine that the work will be more extensive , but I'm ready it's 7:55 we're in the center of the stadium, the teachers are watching us, with dark lenses, that do not indicate where they are going, gentlemen says Professor

Salomomr, today is a great day, we are gathered, to work in the field, with each one of the mental, physical, emotional, teamwork strategies, the priority is the development of activities that complement our adaptation strategies, Professor Yessica will read a manifesto of the challenges that life proposes to us;

Challenges in life

Why? they exist, why? they approach me, why? they confront me

They are learning, they are knowledge, they are wisdom.

If they did not exist, life would be boring, without energy, without meaning.

They enrich my path in life.

They give me philosophy, they teach me the degrees of difficulty that exist.

These are opportunities that give me growth.

They give me an enriched attitude, with strategic solutions.

They can be solved, with the exchange of creative ideas.

They teach you a profile, to face the storms you have in life.

They are crises, which generate difficult merits to collapse.

They produce will to change, enriching.

They teach us that the miracles of solution appear when we least expect it.

By overcoming them, our life becomes more meaningful.

They create champions with leadership.

It makes warriors ready to give their lives.

They show that light embellishes darkness.

They produce changes, which are observed in the course of life.

They produce achievements, individual, group, worldwide.

They teach that perseverance is the attitude towards success.

They show you that being positive, overcomes the negative.

They exercise you, to face the next challenge.

They show us that the bigger the challenge, the bigger the success.

Challenges in life, they show us the path of the seed that you will provide to future generations.

Challenges in life, is the energy that symbolizes the power of realization.

Challenges in life, gives you understanding, cordiality, humanism.

Challenges in life, is the courage used in the projection of a better world.

Challenges in life, is to find yourself and find your strengths.

Challenges in life, is to have the premise of love towards what you do.

Challenges in life, is to dream of the spiritual achievement towards the universe.

Challenges in life, a miracle to dream.

Challenges in life, is a whole, is the whole illusion of Why? Live.

What a great manifesto, indicates a path of great challenges, there are no pretexts to stop, this is a unique learning day, teachers tell us to take each one a bicycle, begins our journey, Professor Yessica, leads the group, the Professor Salomomr goes behind the group, taking care of our path, our determination and our cycling steps, it's great, it's a path of much vegetation, I feel like pure air enters my nostrils, it's a special energy that revives me, I'm living from new, on the way there are waterfalls, lakes, rivers, animals, immense vegetation, it is an earthly paradise, we all take a great step, after an hour of great travel, we went to a super luxury cabin with pools, a waterfall, we hydrated ourselves in that place and we observe the path we have left behind, the teacher tells us to relax 15 minutes hydrate well, we are halfway, after here it is one hour 30 minutes of ascent, for that reason I ask you to fill your lungs with air, take all the necessary liquid, fill the container that you carry on your bicycle.

Professor Yessica speaks, guys I want to congratulate you are great take a good step, continue to strive, we have no pretexts for the great challenge that awaits us, enjoy this great moment of rest, it is a great delight to enjoy this great lapse of recovery time, teachers coordinate the group very well, it's great, the teacher is at the head of the group, there can be some excuse that we can not, the great break ends, ladies and gentlemen ready for the next stage, I ask for your best effort, top awaits us with hydration, great food, massages and hydromassages, waiting for our arrival, the main thing is what they will see arriving at the goal, teacher forward we will begin, the beginning is a hard road, the rise Is prominent the changes in the bicycles they help us a little, they are very modern adaptable for the road, we are going up on slopes not so pronounced, but it seems that they have no end, but I am motivated too much by the smell of the forest. ue, all my senses are fascinated by this great place, are unique experiences that anyone would want in life, it is great to exercise and at the same time enjoy the place where you are, after almost dying by the great effort, all motivated we comply with the goal of that moment, it is great to reach the top, breathe easy, listen to the heartbeat, how our body relaxes and you see it is full of energy, with the satisfaction of having achieved something fabulous.

I turn around slowly 360 degrees observing around me, it is a great island, beautiful, fabulous, it has spectacular buildings, but here at the top they look small, where we arrive is a giant fortress, a modern castle, full of technology , the teacher tells us, gentlemen ahead feel comfortable enjoy this great place they have earned it with their effort and dedication, there are some people who tell us, that we take a bath we climb the elevator on the 9th floor are the bathrooms on the right side of the women, in the background and on the left those of the men, we took a great bath, they told us that on the 18th floor we were going to eat, they are very spacious, the floors are very big rooms, we are in a giant restaurant, we eat fabulously, since we finish indicate us that we went up to the 43rd floor, we arrived and the 44 tells us that it is a rotating restaurant, what a luxury, hopefully and someday we will eat there, on the 43rd floor the teachers will be there, the teacher speaks, we have fulfilled today with our great goal that was to arrive here, our great prize this great place, this indicates that the efforts made bring fabulous rewards, many are short, medium and long term, but there is always ahead of something fantastic and great, everything we learn day after day are experiences that grow over time to become wisdom.

young boys, the teacher speaks, they have an hour to enjoy the luxuries of this place on the 17th floor they will give a fabulous massage in individual whirlpool tubs, after the hour is over I wait for them on the 50th floor where is the helicopter landing area , something unique and great awaits you, see you, enjoy the great moment, we rush to the 17th floor, we enter a fragrant smell, with a combination of nature, the transparent mirrors resemble that we are outside, the view is 360 degrees you can see waterfalls lakes, you can almost see the whole island, they provide us with a fantastic sports massage, which makes us recover our muscles, joints again, after that we went into some whirlpool tubs the latest technology, I almost fell asleep, they indicate us that when there are 15 minutes left for the time a bell will ring, it will indicate that it is time to get ready for the next adventure, we do not know what is waiting for us, we change We hurry to the 50th floor.

We got the place has the capacity of a stadium, the view is amazing, there are our teachers, there are several paragliders with motor, capacity for two people, resemble a helicopter, very advanced technologically, we are about to leave are 14 instructors one for each paraglider, in total are 14 technological birds that circulate through the air, I observe the faces of terror, apparently I am not the only one that has not been thrown in an engine paraglider, suddenly you hear a trembling voice teachers, it is Giselle , I have phobia of heights and I will not participate, the teachers waited a bit to answer, but they said, young people this is part of the class, I promise that if they do it, their mentality will become stronger, but they do not feel forced to carry out this challenge, all decisions are respected, so if I tell them to feel safe that each instructor that goes with you is prepared for any unforeseen 100%, this vehicles have a Auxiliary engine that provides greater security, Giselle if you decide to launch you will do the last, you will see that everything around you is great, teachers I will not also jump into that vehicle, I think we would have been notified of this test, to be visualizing, this it's a surprise that gives me a lot of fear, Winstond life will always give you surprises, situations will happen to you, events you did not expect, so you can say that sometimes it's cruel fate, because it grabs you by surprise, we must be prepared for any event that come to us, but it is your decision that no one will oblige.

Well we start, they are launched one by one, with their respective instructor, the teachers go to Giselle and Winstond, young people and everyone is complying with the protocol, we will be the last to throw ourselves, tell me if they are willing to do it, professors we already talked about doing it, that's why we come to be the best, according Winstond ready, I'm ready to launch with your instructor, then Giselle also does the same with her instructor, each teacher is released, with an instructor, they are 14 paragliding in the sky, the view here is great, you can see the island in its maximum splendor, you can see a lot of vegetation with a touch of futuristic modernity, only the skyscrapers that were made in this place make it unique, my lungs they fill with energy a special and clean air that circulates through my veins, penetrating my heart, I feel alive again, what a magnificent experience it is to fly in paragliding, it teaches us that they exist, c wonderful bears that we need to know, I feel like a free bird, adventurous, knowing this magnificent place, which is full of surprises, that give us learning and experience, we see the 14 paragliders as a single ship in the sky, our distribution , it looks natural, our training resembles a parade of ships, after 1 hour and 15 minutes, we observe a large part of the place, we all have a face of amazement, because of the fantastic location we are in.

We park in a special track, in the middle of the jungle, we all leave the paraglider, together with the instructors, the teacher Yessica tells us to follow her, we arrive at a place full of waterfalls where the water is turquoise blue, indicates the It is a long road, but we have almost finished, our big test today, please invite them to drink water from the waterfall on the right, do not tell me anything until after drinking it, which is what they feel , they start to hear voices, I feel it as a moisturizing drink, it has a different flavor to water I say that because of the minerals it has, I feel a lot of energy, I feel happy, happy, healthy, young people this waterfall has the name ¨la strength and youth¨, anyone who feels some disease, the natural compounds that it has, relieves them and frees them of any health problem, if this water were marketed, it would make people immensely rich, but the owners of the to island, do not want to do business, with this part of nature, young people have achieved this day unique experiences, I want you to listen to this thought;

The mentality is alive

When I face the obstacles that come my way, I realize that I am alive.

When I fight for what I want, my heart beats strong, filling me with energy.

When my goals are obstructed by obstacles, I realize the value.

I dream of my goal, my insight brings me closer to him, but I know that more is missing.

My visualization gives me strength to continue my path.

I have fallen several times, the blows have been so strong that many times I have thought not to continue.

The mentality is alive, it indicates without strength that I continue on my way.

That inner voice gives me life, gives me energy, gives me a map of the road to continue.

The mentality is alive, it teaches me that there is a special path where defeat does not exist.

It's when you dare to be spectacular things you never imagined.

Transcend in the story doing great things where courage and decision form a single link.

The mentality is alive, because every day is a new day, that the greatest effort is the premise.

When you fight and your strength increases, tiredness disappears, the mentality is alive.

If you enjoy what you do, fatigue does not reach your mind.

If you enjoy what you do, without expecting anything in return, the universe will reward you.

If you enjoy what you do with love and decision a light will illuminate your path, there will be no more darkness.

If you enjoy what you do, you will give meaning to your life, you will know why you are in the world.

The mentality is alive, your tranquility with which you assume challenges teaches you to dream.

The mentality is alive, because you have a fabulous machine worthy of appreciating that it is your body.

The mentality is alive, because the universe is witness that your goal will contribute to the development.

The mentality is alive, because your sensations make you be alive and fully enjoy what surrounds you.

The mentality is alive, because it is in connection with you and the universe.

The mentality is alive, because it makes you dream, you know that every day is unique.

The mentality is alive, it helps you to live to the fullest.

The mentality is alive, with the universe ready to make your dreams come true.

The mentality is alive, the spirit, the love, the universe are one.

The mentality is alive.

As the teacher finishes mentioning the great thought, Professor Salomomr, guys it is important that each one of you, in all your classes, give yourselves to the maximum, the thought that the teacher shows us is full of real philosophy, in all its projects should use 1,2,3,4,5 the necessary efforts, when we finish the last crossing, I will comment on this great philosophy, well the next obstacle is to swim in the course of the river to the lake, are approximately 1,000 meters or a 1 kilometer, on the shore we wait for the whole group, good guys ahead, we all go into the river, we are swimming is fabulous, the water feels fresh, after a while, we met the goal and everyone gathered.

The teacher tells us, young people the bicycles, that you see, each one is personalized with your name, they are the ones that started the trip in the morning, we are going to continue the last journey, and on the way back it is downhill, with a few earrings , Professor Yessica will go in front of the group, I will do it last, all in line guys, go ahead, oh my God, I do not know where I get so much strength, but I feel fabulous, like a child who does not get tired and can play everything the day will be the water of the waterfall or the mentality, I do not know but I feel fabulous, after a long journey of almost an hour, we are arriving after appreciating the great nature, the great place we are, the earthly treasure that we belongs for as long as we are, I feel fantastic, because I live in a big city, I do not have a paradise like this, our goal was again the stadium, we can call our second home of operations for our personal development, all is We're meeting, the teacher, young people, I'm going to talk to you;

The effort 1, 2, 3,4 ...

When I have struggled to excel, my self-esteem has been strengthened.

The obstacles have taught me, the value of the goals.

The sweat, the tears, the failure, have taught me to appreciate my achievements.

The present has been my priority, today is the most important thing in my life.

Every step I take, I feel it, I live it to the fullest, because I know it will not come back.

Every day is different, full of infinite riches of unique experiences.

The effort taught me not to give up, to give my best without waiting for a prize.

When I was defeated, I am left with the breath of the last effort and those that were necessary.

Let the universe be a witness, that the last effort was my companion.

That the last effort taught me never to give up.

I am a warrior, effort 1, 2, 3,4 ... They are my weapons, against the decision, the defeat, the uncertainty.

I am not afraid, he effort 1, 2, 3,4 .... He accompanies me in my storms.

The effort that is necessary to achieve my goal gives me strength.

My philosophy never to give up, to be satisfied that I did my best.

I know that if I use the formula of maximum effort the result will not matter, because the universe will witness my mental strength.

My satisfaction will be full that I will never give up.

The effort 1, 2, 3,4 ... those that are necessary to transcend.

The effort 1, 2, 3,4 ... love, spirituality is the satisfaction of being a warrior.

I own the effort 1, 2, 3,4 ... they belong to me.

The effort 1, 2, 3,4 ... It is the magic to bury the pretexts.

The effort 1, 2, 3,4 ... It is to surrender the maximum without waiting for the results, the happiness, the smile of the duty fulfilled.

Young is for me and the teacher to have a group as valuable as you, I thank you, have done your work with effort, mentality, heart, spirituality, it is important to manage a profile with these characteristics is the key of any place , of any project, of any achievement, I congratulate you, it is a privilege, to have a group, with these characteristics, we are finished, have an excellent day and a pleasant Sunday, I leave you with some words of Professor Yessica, guys like the professor said it, they are a great group, they show it with their dedication, everything they did, they did it with passion, love, courage, these manifestations give them a personality full of competence, all the athletes in the world have those characteristics as bases, keep fighting day by day, surrendering yourself to the maximum, for being exemplary people, for achieving your goals and objectives, having wonderful days, I wait for you in the following c lase, we retire with a special joy, the words, the philosophies that the professors transmit, reach our hearts, it is fantastic, as each class lives with an eternal spirituality and a magnificent connection, as if we already knew each other for a long time, it will be that we join, because we all seek the same goal, everything that has happened these days makes me admire every day more all the people around me, it is something magnificent, difficult to explain, but it is felt from the heart, it is a spiritual, unique connection.

We are going to our Yoga Bioenergetics class we are in the classroom at 5:55 pm, as the day has gone by very quickly, but with fantastic experiences, Professor Noetherli, tells us to take the position she has, we sit in in front of her we are in lotus flower, young people close their eyes, breathe deeply, exhale slowly, feel the oxygen flow as it enters through your body turning it into energy, I want you to relive the most painful feeling that you have had, keep breathing In the same way with energy, there is pain in their bodies, take out that pain, if they cry, relive that painful moment, keep breathing, I listen to that pain, I feel your pain, look for an alternative solution for that fact and if it does not exist, relive that moment to the maximum without fear, now I want you to remember the most beautiful thing that has happened to them, revívanlo, that their faces are illuminated, that positive energy fill this place, very well guys enjoy In this great moment, slowly open your eyes, realize that we can handle in an instant our emotions whether negative or positive, we live in such a way as if they were real or as if they were happening at this time, emotions negative are a heavy burden that often do not let us continue our way, there are disturbing emotions, which have occurred many years ago and we live with such reality as if they were happening instantly, listen to this thought that penetrates your heart.

Negative emotions

That transport us to the past, living horror movies.

Time does not matter, you can live them instantly, they affect you at the moment.

It is a heavy burden, which does not let you continue.

You fight day by day to forget them and the opposite happens, they appear constantly.

Do not fight to forget them, revive them when necessary.

They are living scars, that will hurt you, but that, with time, with frequency, the pain will disappear.

Your negative emotions will be assimilated by your mind, where the manifested pain will be reduced.

Terror invades you, your persuasion for forgetting, makes coexistence more frequent.

You must circulate according to the current of your life, if you fight against it, it will never disappear.

Negative emotion will envelop you in your terror if you keep avoiding it.

If you face it with courage, it will hurt, it will be an excruciating pain, which will diminish over time.

Be brave do not fight against the negative emotion, feel the pain, it will diminish, the time will help you.

When your mind assimilates all the negative information and makes it part of you, it will be a relief because the fear will disappear.

You have fled from pain for a long time, today you face it, you feel better.

Today you are brave, your vision increases, your reflexes improve, your strength grows.

Negative emotions, they are scars that followed you, that affected you, that almost destroyed you.

Negative emotions, which taught you to grow, taught you to observe that life is not easy.

Negative emotions, which taught you to take control of your life, living each day to the fullest, adding to your life negative and positive experiences.

You own your emotions, the balance teaches you that emotions complement your life.

The scars taught you to grow in pain, in the face of failure, in the face of tears, in the face of suffering.

Your strength will give you understanding, to live the negative and positive to the maximum, so that it is not buried in the past.

You have the solution, that the negative emotion is buried in the place that belongs to it.

Do not be afraid of a negative emotion, live it to the maximum, feel the pain.

Time will heal your scar, pain may present itself, but with less intensity.

You own your emotions, live them to the maximum, no matter their value.

Young people analyze what they heard, in the descriptive memory that they tell about each of their classes, they will find all the thoughts, that their professors show them, when they have time to analyze them, they will find infinity of wisdom that they can use in the great journey of their life, when we started the class they felt the power of emotions, they realized that negatives destroy us, but they can also be constructive, teaching us self-defense, in the face of pain, they teach us as children not to express our emotions, not to cry, not to be sad, we all like to be happy and avoid negative emotions at all costs, but it is important to manifest all our emotions, they will make us stronger and more aware of what happens around us, we are owners of our emotions even if they are negative, young people have finished the class, I invite you to reflect, to be observers of the reality of life, we all wish emotions positive, but without the negatives, the experience and the learning before the pain, it would diminish our strengths, continue on your way, with great success, rest, relax, enjoy your great moments, which are unique.

What a wonderful class, if it is true we want our life to be full of many positive things and negative ones give us a lot of pain, when we can avoid them, that is why they do not disappear, the more you avoid something, the more you are buried in your mind, now if to rest that big day, well as always I will observe the monitor to see if someone resorts to the guru Taoci, a moment passes and suddenly on the screen appears Giselle and Winstond, they go to see the guru, they arrive at the temple , a spiritual voice is heard, young boys I know they have come, but I want them to express their feelings from the depths of their hearts.

Daughter I hear you, today I was very afraid to perform the paragliding test, it was even my fear, I refused to do it, the teachers at all times supported me with their understanding, but they told me not to give up, it was such My fear that I decided to leave this great project, but came to my mind infinity of things and one of them was to face fear, I had a hard time being in this great project, because I was going to give up so easily, I pass the face of my mother, my father, my brothers, her tears when I left her side, wishing me the best, it was something great that came to my mind at that time of crisis.

Daughter in this life we have many tests that often prevent us from continuing our journey, it is essential always daughter, face with courage to what comes your way, that gives you more strength, when you face the problems, the experience you get is manifested in your achievements, everyone in this life has fears, we even feel fear of things that often never manifest, they are precepts that we have in our imagination, we create a world of obstacles that when we face them, we observe that the majority did not happen, our mentality it is so strong that often imaginary obstacles affect the path of our lives, daughter this day you have learned something, that just as the obstacles are in your mind, also the solutions, the motivations are in your mind, your family that appeared Suddenly, it was a manifestation of the motivational defenses, of which you are the owner, your struggles for something, for someone, manifest it in your anti e the obstacle that presents itself to you.

Life gives you many experiences and learning, it is important to be a great observer during your journey, observe, analyze, understand your body, your mental defenses, which enrich your path, thank you very much Guru illuminate me with your words, if daughter many times that we do not imagine it we have the solution, to the problems that are presented to us, Winstond I listen to you, Mr. Guru happened to me something similar to Giselle, a fear crossed me throughout my body that paralyzed me, left me speechless, I only told the teachers that no, it was the only word that came out of my mind, it was so much my fear that my vision blurred, I only remembered the accident that my father had when jumping from a parachute and that left him paralytic, all the suffering that we went through came to my mind, I thought the worst before getting on the paraglider, I said if it happens to me the same as my father, it is an extreme suffering, a pain that accompanies me forever is difficult to remove it e my mind, manifests you must in time, in the last class was very important for me, Professor

Noetherli spoke to us precisely about the negative emotions and how they affect us, how they distort our life, how it is a heavy burden, which does not stop our way, all that the teacher mentioned are the manifestations that I felt, it was a problem of my father that affected the whole family, I say forever.

My father died, but we feel the heavy burden of the problem on our shoulders, if the child feels the pain you transmit, the pain you feel, our mind is very powerful, it can create health or otherwise diseases, as the teacher said it is important to leave flow emotions, do not go against the current events that occur in life are full of learning, often pain, gives us learning, gives us tools how to deal with the pain, our loved ones during the duel they mention us , that we forget, on the contrary our defense mechanisms, it is important to face the pain manifesting it, feeling the heartbreaking suffering, until the time is the great witness, of the pain reduction, when you manifest it, that pain diminishes its frequency , because your body is the healer, you have a deep understanding of what you are going through.

Like Giselle you faced a devastating obstacle, but you came out triumphant because you faced it, I know that it was very difficult for you to accept the challenge in the best way, but that challenge gave you greatness, it made you stronger, life as I commented to Giselle, presents you with many challenges, you must be aware that the road to success is not easy, you have to suffer, fall, fail, so that all this pain lived, make you appreciate the success achieved, if everything in this life were easy, you would not give them the value that the achievements deserve, when you achieve your goals, you have battled, you have been about to surrender and you continue your constant struggle, that gives you more courage, willingness to face the next challenge or be aware that during your Journey you will face different difficulties, that even delay your way.

I am happy because this day was full of much learning for the two of you, I teach you that when facing obstacles, you have another perspective of life, your fears, your failures, even imaginary situations, will avoid your path, the important thing is to realize of the power of our positive mind, a mentality where to achieve an achievement or to reach the desired goal, the road will be full of obstacles, but if you maintain the mentality that you presented today, it will be the antecedent that will motivate you to achieve what you set out on the great path of your life, all your projects will be difficult but you will always have the initiative to think that no obstacle will make you fall, the positive mentality you got this day, put together the puzzle of tools that will will give power, courage, before what is presented to them, children be spiritual, address themselves through love, do with pleasure, joy, everything that comes their way , enjoy what they do, show passion, sow a seed, cultivate it with dedication, love, so that the fruit you give is fantastic, magnificent, unique, that expresses every detail, every persuasion, pain, crying, that they manifested, before to achieve your goal, enjoy the triumph, be alive, use all your senses in the manifestations of nature itself, be perceptive to what surrounds you.

Be positive, join people who resemble you in thought, mentality, convictions, this will make them grow forever and will show future generations that this life is full of immensity of wonders that often have no cost, the only cost is to enjoy them with energy and passion, children rest live every day to the fullest, obtain the wisdom that is transmitted to them, be great observers of what happens around them, this will make them great individuals, great leaders, rest dream of a better world , your interior is fantastic, the exterior does not affect you, you only take the best, the great experiences that life gives you.

What great words of Guru Taoci, it is a special learning, it is a philosophical learning, every intervention that manifests, it does it with a special power, a real power, I realize that I am missing countless things to learn, that the path of life has many surprises, the learning we receive daily, we often let it go, the important thing is to be great observers, what happens around us, analyze the information we receive, to be better individuals, each person is only, but often their problems are similar to those of others, even solutions can have similarities, emotional behaviors lead us to enter the spirituality of being, which manifests our states of control, whether positive or negative, be attentive observers of what happens around us gives us more tools to face the problems that come our way, well it's time to sleep was a unique day, ma ravilloso and special, full of learning, courage, recognition of ideas, a great spirituality.

CHAPTER IV

The classes have been fabulous, we all have a different perspective of when we arrived, tomorrow Saturday is the big day of the first evaluation of the whole group, the first participant will leave, tomorrow we will be a month away from here, how fast time has passed , I feel stronger, more focused, more awake, more intelligent, this program has awakened all our senses, the exchange of ideas, has made in us, a unique and special feedback, the one that leaves this place will have another perspective different, it will be a better leader, it will have the necessary tools to face the challenges that arise, I am not the same, I imagine that the judges, wish that nobody retired, but if it were like that it would not be a competition to look for the best project of the world, to benefit the population that needs it the most.

The main judges will be the professors who, according to their evaluations, will have the great responsibility of eliminating the first competitor, it is a difficult job, I would say very difficult, but necessary for the development of the project, tomorrow Saturday will be the great day that one of the participants will leave this great place, who will be, it is difficult to know, because they are all great leaders, willing to be the greatest sacrifice to achieve their goals.

It's 20:20 I can not be quiet I watch the line of monitors and nobody assists with the Guru, I have a great need to go see him, talk with him, express my concerns, take a deep breath, I go to the temple, he's in a mountain, it is splendid to climb, fill the lungs with fresh air and hear the beating of my heart, it is fascinating to go to the temple, the air is fresh, I come to the temple in the shadows the guru leaves, son waited for you, do not hesitate to approach me , I also need to listen to you, guru Taoci, I am fascinated with this place and at the same time grateful that I have been allowed to be part of the group of participants, they have been indescribable teachings, a world of constructive life, unique, special, but great Lord, I am restless pensive, I have the responsibility that I have over my shoulders, I am happy to belong to this great project, but I am worried, tomorrow the activity is suspended, to know who is the one who is leaving, is something very difficult to express, it is a nostalgic feeling that invades me, the great person that retires from here, as it is going to take, I have observed infinity of happy faces, of all the participants, it is great to observe that spark of achievement that has each participant, is a surprising duel that we will suffer all the members of this project to see a participant depart.

Son I understand your feelings, but it is important in some cases to be strong, the benefits that are being sought are worldwide, the participants are aware of the competition, the effort they make daily will be rewarded in the stay of the place, they know that if not they do things as they should, they are risking their place in the group, due to the great responsibility of the project only one will be the winner, always when there is a loss there is nostalgia from which it goes, to those who were close to the character, life is full of duels of all kinds, the important thing is to accept it, to know that the sacrifices that are made are to benefit the population in the world, son always observes the benefits, understanding will come little by little, you know the great responsibility of being Here, in any competition you have to see a winner, we know that the winner will benefit the world with his project, this project teaches us a great proposal that everyone will be We are winners.

As a priority the leadership, love, spirituality, commitment, humanity, first of all forever, the universe is witness to the manifestation of positive spirituality that surrounds us, great guru is a privilege to talk with you, I feel calm, I needed talk, my mentality continues to grow, I look forward to tomorrow, it will be a great day that will transcend history as a legacy for future generations, you know great guru, I am amazed to belong to this great project, son rests, relax tomorrow a great day awaits us, we must wait with enthusiasm and energy, rest son.

I retire I am going down the mountain and at the same time thinking the great comments of the great guru, it is true in life that sacrifices have to be made and if they are for a world benefit, it is important to accept them with efficiency and determination. I feel calmer, I will rest in wonder, waiting for the big day tomorrow, the teachers I think they will not sleep at 3:00 pm they will have to say who is the one who leaves this fantastic place, tomorrow is his third day of meeting, for the evaluations, we hope the best results, they are great teachers will know how to choose, the great leader who retires.

It's Saturday, it's 2:30 pm. I'm headed to the great hall, which will witness the big event, which is about to begin, we get into some luxurious cars, we go to the great hall, it is located on a mountain with marble steps around it, as a great monument, farewell, the retiring competitor, we are gathered in the room, the professors are facing us in the big panel, surrounded by three giant screens, take the floor, I am Professor Curielm Scientist, Philosopher, Psychologist, I am part of this great project as all my colleagues who are here present; Mission, eliminate world poverty, on behalf of my colleagues manifest the great job that was to select the great leader who has to retire, then I am going to present you with great images of all of you, of your great work during the month, I see the images They are great, all the work we have done is manifested in this great recording, indeed there were many tears when observing the images, I turn to see everyone and know that one is the one who is going to go, it is difficult, but it is a great competition, the great documentary ends.

Continue Professor Curielm, the world is transformed day by day, technology is modernized, minds are grouped to achieve innovations that represent them in the future, master minds are aware of the changes, information runs around the world in short periods of time, the person who retires, has to be happy and satisfied, to have been in a great place and to take into account that all the participants were selected worldwide, there were many individuals who wished to belong to this project, I thank for the courage to struggle during this month to achieve the path to success, during our life there will be obstacles, setbacks, failures that will often impede our path, the important thing is to visualize, other alternatives that help us achieve our dreams, sometimes our roads are diverted, our roads are not uncertain, they teach us, they give us experiences, learning, ways of acting in the face of storms s, they are all winners from the moment they stepped on this place, it is significant, imagine the person who retires is among the twelve best in the world, it is gratifying their participation, their contribution to this great project, it is necessary, the person who is withdraw from this place, continue with his legacy, the struggle is day by day, the only final defeat is death.

In the way of life, battles are lost, that if we analyze them, they leave us gains, that is experience, to learn from failures, it is important for our formation, this great experience that you lived in this great place is unique and incomparable, but our path continues, we have a great responsibility, which weighs on our shoulders, makes us walk slowly, but decisively, with strength, with energy, with our heads held high, our project ¨Mision, eliminate world poverty¨ we are a team, the person who leaves, will support us spiritually, with his strength, we will imagine that he is with us, but we know clearly that there will only be one winner, for me and for all the teachers, it has been 3 days of intense evaluations, they are great competitors , the one who left was for a small fault, because in reality they are all great world leaders, the competitor that retires, leaves satisfied, to have fulfilled a great job, the prize was a great month full of experiences and learning, the person who withdraws from this place forever is the number competitor:

7.- Name: Akiakv

Age: 38 years

Country: Alaska

Profession: Industrial Engineer

Project: create industries that facilitate food

Sport: Ice skating

Language: English, French, Russian

Altruism for the world: the development of industries to feed the world, with products that are easy to transport and that expire in 10 years.

Say goodbye to your teammates and wish them the best of luck, your great work was essential for this great group. The whole group cries a great companion is gone, it is a great loss, productive for the group, we know the great responsibility, only one will be the winner, will be the ambassador of all the masterminds, of all the learning that has been obtained during this journey, full of riches and wisdom, goodbye hurts, but life has to continue, projects have to continue, there are 11 competitors and a long way to go, Akiakv retires through a tunnel full of light, goes to the guru Taoci, it's your last talk with him, it's scheduled at 5:00 p.m., it will give me time to listen to your great talk.

The teacher finalizes her speech, competitors, receive a cordial greeting from all her teachers, asking them for their total dedication, in this great project, fight day after day, with determination, until the last effort, a new day emerges in their paths, the triumph yesterday was a breath, today is a different day, fight every moment, that your strength is expressed in your motivation to continue your way, you know that you are being evaluated, fight to be the best, enjoy what you do, feel alive, you are part of the universe, your project will benefit the most vulnerable people, the people who decide a change in their life, the global era will witness the great event we are experiencing, continue your journey, I am your teacher Curielm.

We all retired a little sad, but at the same time know the competitors, who must strive every day more, if they can not be the next one to retire, it is an intense pressure seen in the faces of the competitors, but at the same time they belong to something great that will give another profile to their lives, everyone knows from the time they are here their lives have changed 360 degrees, their work as the next leaders of the world will be manifested day by day, I go to my house, I go straight to the monitors, I am interested to know what goes through the mind of Akiakv, before this great event in his life, I am interested to know how he took his departure.

A voice is heard Guru Taoci, tell me son you need, I know that during the month I was here, never visit you, but today I feel devastated, finished, I do not want to leave, I get used to this beautiful place, to the great coexistence, that I had with my classmates, the classes, the teachers, the food, everything I will miss I am devastated Guru, son I know how you feel, but this is a contest of great responsibility, to save the most needy people in the world, your way was great, this month take it as a great adventure of great learning, the process was wonderful, son when you are presented in life the best desserts, or what is delicious for you, the time comes that you do not enjoy it as if it were the first time, your stay here was a great dessert, I finish the dessert, you have a great way, follow the course of your river of opportunities, do not go against the current, live the day as if it were the last, enjoy things, as if Do not be with you again, I Every day imagining a loss, to enjoy every moment to the fullest, your karma is fabulous, your delivery in what you propose, manifests in your success, but in that way there will be failures, life is not pure bliss, there are setbacks , stumbles, fears, struggles without prizes, the important thing is the experience you get day by day, the ease with which you develop in life is a priority, that you must manifest at every moment.

Take the important events in your life as learning, the great school of life will teach you that when you get what you want, you will be grateful, you will receive the prizes, like a great warrior who gave the last drop of encouragement, to achieve their goals and objectives, feel happy for the place you stepped on, for the great experience you experienced, the world does not end, this is just the beginning of what awaits you in life, go on your way with your head held high, dreaming, creating, innovating, making what you propose, with love, dedication, enjoyment, feel the happiness of each step you take, love your loved ones, fight for them, leave in your life a legacy that you never surrendered, that you fell, but you turned to lift, you failed, but at the same time you learned how not to be things, failures fill you with experience, always seek what is most precious in life is true knowledge, is great wisdom.

Thank you very much great Guru, you have awakened me, I feel alive again, willing to continue fighting to achieve my goals, a door was closed, I am willing to continue playing countless doors, until it opens, with which I have always dreamed, great guru, thank you for your wisdom, for your words of encouragement, I leave happy, because I know that my spirit stays in this great place, to support my colleagues to keep fighting, until it comes out, the great winner, who your courage, will represent us, son give me a hug, I fill you with energy with my good vibes, always fight, go the way of the winners, your positive thoughts, fill your mind and wherever you go be your profile of presentation, feel happy, you gave your best effort, my blessings are with you, thank you guru Taoci, I retire, with energy and happiness.

Akiakv retires, calm, with another face, like a great leader, willing to fight to achieve his goals, I am amazed, the magic that has and wisdom, Taoci guru, all who have turned to him, we know his magic, of his understanding, of the breath, he makes us see things in a great way, as if he entered our minds, I know he is our spiritual guide, but I am surprised at the motivation he manifests, towards the people who visit him. There are 11 competitors and a long way to go, here I have the agenda of the subjects that we will take in the following month;

Monday	Teacher	Subject
8:00 to 10:45	Salomomr	Physical and mental training II
11:00 to 12:45	Laeva	Global Leadership II
12:50 to 13:50	FOOD	

| 14:00 to 15:45 | Teslac | Innovation II |

| 16:00 to 17:45 | McYuretzili | Communication and understanding II |

| 18:00 to 18:55 | Edisonic | Transcendental Ideas II |

| 19:00 to 20:00 | Noetherli | Yoga Bioenergetics II |

Tuesday	**Teacher**	**Subject**
8:00 to 10:45	Salomomr	Sports Philosophy and Training II
11:00 to 12:45	Markl	Human Development II
12:50 to 13:50	FOOD	
14:00 to 15:45	Vincir	Creatividad II
16:00 to 17:45	Curielm	Motivation II
18:00 to 18:55	Yessica	Positive Mentality II
19:00 to 20:00	Noetherli	Yoga Bioenergetics II

Wednesday	**Teacher**	**Subject**
8:00 to 10:45	Yessica	Training special forces II
11:00 to 12:45	Laeva	Global Leadership II
12:50 to 13:50	FOOD	

14:00 to 15:45	Teslac	Innovation II
16:00 to 17:45	McYuretzili	Communication and understanding II
18:00 to 18:55	Edisonic	Transcendental Ideas II
19:00 to 20:00	Noetherli	Yoga Bioenergetics II

Thursday	**Teacher**	**Subject**
8:00 to 10:45	Salomomr	Sports Philosophy and Training II
11:00 to 12:45	Markl	Human Development II
12:50 to 13:50	FOOD	
14:00 to 15:45	Vincir	Creatividad II
16:00 to 17:45	Curielm	Motivation II
18:00 to 18:55	Yessica	Positive Mentality II
19:00 to 20:00	Noetherli	Yoga Bioenergetics II

Friday	**Teacher**	**Subject**
8:00 to 10:45	Salomomr	Physical and mental training II
11:00 to 12:45	Markl	Communication II
12:50 to 13:50	FOOD	
14:00 to 15:45	Vincir	Creatividad II

| 16:00 to 17:45 | Curielm | Motivation II |

| 18:00 to 18:55 | Yessica | Positive Mentality II |

| 19:00 to 20:00 | Noetherli | Yoga Bioenergetics II |

Saturday	**Teacher**	**Subject**
8:00 to 17:45	Salomomr	Training Exploration Forces
	Yessica	Specials II
18:00 to 20:00	Noetherli	Yoga Bioenergetics II

Sunday

Strategic rest; with work options according to the needs of the participant.

Important note:

All the subjects are focused, with the project of each competitor.

waiting for the day Monday, to start a new adventure, this month that happened was fabulous, full of great experiences, that have given me more knowledge, it has been very necessary and important, belong to the group, do what each of the competitors realize, gives me understanding of the great process, of the great knowledge that the professors transmit, the knowledge is a great treasure, that helps us to acquire the necessary experience, for our development in real life, my instance in this wonderful place, It has been a great construction, that in a short time, I will be using the great training that I have received.

I thank God for allowing me to be in this place, where I am receiving wonderful gifts, that will contribute to the most precious thing that we all want in the world, to have the great wisdom, what a fantastic analysis of this month's journey, I imagine that the competitors, they have thoughts similar to mine, you can see every day how they give themselves to the exercises, to the studies transmitted by the teachers, every detail is important, that has given them a great perspective, of their project, for global benefit, they know which is a great competition, all the participants are trained to win, it is difficult to know the next one to leave, since I know, that next month will be stronger, because no one wants to leave and I recognize, it is a great place of dreams, that any researcher of the world, any scientist, any leader of the world or of history, would have wished to have a place like this, with the meeting of all the necessary characteristics for a great development, where the best teachers in the world, are our mentors, who transmit, their knowledge, experiences, philosophy, wisdom, training, it is great to have all the development tools necessary to achieve a desired goal, we breathe a healthy, spiritual group environment, real competition, unprecedented experiences, which are forming a great profile, a profile of global development, the great day of Sunday ended, it was a great day of rest, reflection, analysis, consideration, spirituality, knowing what what awaits the great competitors, we have to say, that great great days await us, that will leave a mark, in our minds, in our spirit, in our hearts, I will rest, to wait for the new day Monday, the new project will begin of the month.

Monday starting day, it is great to wake up to a new day, without knowing what you expect, the great background, of the last month, shows me that something wonderful, great, unique awaits us, classes continued, I found in each competitor a new perspective , a new beginning, it is difficult to know the next one that will go away, everyone has a thirst for triumph that can be seen in his face, in his actions, it is a huge energy, that has come out with force to shine, from what I see, the rhythm of competition is great, nobody wants to leave, everyone is very participative, you see that your project is in their soul and their hearts, the evaluations of the teachers have to be stronger, the level has gone up too much, I realize that when there are competitions, it is when courage arises, to be a leader, it is a unique combination of ideas, this learning that I am experiencing, you do not get it that easy, it is a treasure that I will always thank, never finish one of learning, every day is an experience differently, every day leaves you a teaching, that serves you as a formation and that you will use when you least expect it, wisdom, knowledge, has always been desired, by the great cultures of all times, by the great historical leaders , wisdom is a unique treasure, it is Saturday the week has been fantastic, of great competitors, great teachers, the light of knowledge shines.

I watch the monitor, there is a little light that tells me that someone will see the guru Taoci, the great guru has a lot of spiritual philosophy, it is a great privilege, to have a person, who supports us in times of crisis, the monitor appears Florecent, sr. Guru, a light appears from the dark, tell me daughter, I'm here to help you, I thought a lot about visiting you, but it's something I can not avoid, you know, tell me, speak with your heart, I'm here to listen to you, everything I'm living in these moments is something unique, fantastic, beautiful, a dream come true, coexistence with my classmates, my teachers, I see them as my family, it is such a human, so balanced environment, I feel in a wonderful place, but in my mind The face of my father, his terminal illness, affected me forever, the pain of my mother, my brothers, I feel it in my heart, it is a pain, that is in my whole body, I have always asked God, because we all this happens, my father is good, a great person, who deserves to be happy, we have suffered so much, we have had my father's disease in our bowels, it has been 10 years of full suffering, which affects our path in life, it affects our illusions, we almost do not smile Yes, we have lost the magic of enjoying, laughing, dreaming, pain is very strong, is unbearable.

If daughter I feel your pain, I go through your mind, be your days of suffering, I know that to be here you have made too many sacrifices, I know that your mind, is with your parents, you are making superhuman efforts, to keep fighting, even daughter, I knew that you thought you would be eliminated from the competition, but what if you should know that if you continue in this place is for something, your parents, your whole family, are happy, that you belong to a great project, life is difficult, complicated, not everything is happiness, I know that those ten years have been stormy for you, your path has been too difficult, you feel pain for the suffering of your loved ones, you wish you had a great life, where the terror of the disease disappeared, There are times when it is best to resign ourselves, to what happens and leave everything in the hands of God, through life, we have failures, great setbacks, sufferings, some form us, make us stronger, others destroy us, but we have we continue, after the storms comes the calm, that calm, that gives you rest, recovery of energy, analysis of ideas, experience, knowing that when positive situations arise you must be grateful, enjoy them to the fullest, If I say to you daughter, who continues with your training, keep fighting to the fullest, strive every day, that big problem that is stuck in your mind, you will receive the light and surprise of a great miracle that will change the course of your life and the one of your loved ones.

Daughter miracles exist, many times when you do not find a way out, you do not find a solution to a problem, you feel that there is no other remedy, there is the great light that illuminates your heart, that gives you the courage to keep going, the most precious thing comes, the great miracle, that you imagined that it would never happen, daughter life is full of surprises, you ask what you want with spirituality and love, the surprise of changes in your life, can arise when you least expect it, when you least expect it, when you have found all the doors closed of the blessings, that heavenly door will come inviting you to pass, you will be fully enlightened and that light will reach your loved ones, daughter do not stop your path, those 10 years have been of sufferings, wait for happiness, you must be ready when that great moment arrives, the universe will witness your full happiness, each step will strengthen you, each step will teach you, that only, you should be grateful for the great moments that you will They will come to your life.

Thanks forever, change your life and do what you've always dreamed, daughter cries do not hide your emotions, over time your heart will understand that your pain has healed and that pain will diminish, until it no longer affects your path, all that pain it will become something positive that will make you stronger forever, thank you great guru, you have awakened in me a great hope, knowing that hope must die to the last, fills me with energy, gives me a fascinating awareness that many times it can reach the biggest thing I hope, the great miracle of being happy and that my loved ones also enjoy that great dream, thank you great guru, today I realize, I needed to talk to you, I am happy to have expressed my pain, I felt like a It stuck in my chest, which affected my path.

If you are right, I will never stop fighting, as long as the strength and energy is in me, I will not stop fighting, I feel very happy in this place and I know that my family is happy, because I know I belong to a fabulous project, it is an achievement that we all celebrate together, daughter rests, relax, enjoy the great moments you are living, because they are unique and will not come back, you have the ability to be a great leader, a great example of future generations, the seed that you are cultivating , will be fruit for countless people who are forever grateful, great words will be written in your legacy, where your dedication, your discipline, your love for what you do, your pain will diminish over time, your maturity , will teach you that there are fascinating things in life, that the only thing that remains is to enjoy them, your family is a great base to your life, they will have the joy of seeing you forever with an admiration, that motivates them to follow forward, you are her support, you are her strength, fight forever daughter, give yourself to the maximum, the power to achieve your goals, life smiles, awaits the big surprises that life will give you, the most precious will come to you, as the great miracle you've waited forever, daughter rests and you know you have me, thank you great guru, stamped his thanks with a big sincere hug, that anecdotes of life I am amazed, of what each person brings in his mind, faces we observe, hearts do not know what they contain, we see an infinity of people and we do not know what they have, their problems, what affects them, the life stories, they give us reflection, that people struggle to achieve happiness, to have nice emotions that let you enjoy life.

The third week is Saturday, today we have the great subject. Training Exploration Special Forces II are 7:45 am I go to the meeting point, the great stadium that awaits us, our teachers, observe us with dark glasses, impatient for the great work What we are about to do, says Professor Salomomr, competitors today is a great day, a new day that will witness our skills, the mentality we have, today competitors, we will do a triathlon, which consists of 3 stages;

1.- Swimming 1,500 meters.

2.- Bicycle 40 kilometers

3.- Race 10 Kilometers

Competitors any question or clarification I am to resolve it, raise the hand Rosalinda competitor, if ahead tell me, professor I want to know, well I agree that we must exercise to be healthy, but I think a triathlon is too much, just thinking about the distances, it is something difficult to fulfill, exact competitor Rosalinda, if in this life things were easy, anyone would have the determination to do them, in reality, this is a place to compete, you are evaluated in all the matters, your strengths, they depend on the sport, when they leave here they will find in their path an infinity of challenges, that often they are presented without imagining them, they must be prepared, for every step they take in life, life will not always treat them wonderfully, there will be occasions , that the failures throw them to the ground, the positive power of their self-esteem will raise them, the courage with which you count will be a necessary tool for I continue to follow your path, I invite you competitors to strive, life is what asks you strength, determination, courage, when you face different challenges in your life, you feel fuller, more alive.

Triathlon is a sport too complete, I am looking for you athletes of high performance, to develop a physical base, to make them in this competition elite athletes, athletes of special forces, to serve this great training, I answer to everybody; will provide them with an athlete profile, a positive, clinging and strong mentality, a philosophical attitude towards real life of what they are living, living each day to the fullest, discipline, tenacity, achievement mentality, self-realization, high self-esteem, a healthy body, full of energy, spirituality, connection with the universe, satisfaction of fulfilling goals and objectives, personality, health, countless other things that will help you to transcend in your great way around the world, with you the teacher Yessica, competitors As they listened to the teacher, the exercise is full of benefits, a fortiori the Exploration Special Forces Training II, next I am going to read this parchment called;

Challenge

I looked at the sun and I realized how far it is from me, but its energy strengthens me.

On my way I regret for the failures and mistakes, instead of taking advantage of all the options that have been presented to me.

My laments created insecurity in my mind, torment me with what never happened.

I thought that tomorrow was great to start, but I forgot that time was passing.

I dreamed of a wonderful future, forgetting about the present, forgetting that it was the construction of my life.

My life was full of illusions, they were castles in the air, without bases, without structure.

My scars from the past, they torment me, they have been part of my present, they are still open.

My reflection looked for alternatives, I looked for a sense of life.

Until the light came to my life, illuminated my whole body, illuminated my spirit, illuminated my heart.

I get the challenge to my life, I get strength, courage.

Challenge, that every time you introduce yourself I feel alive, my illusions return.

I challenge, that you approach me to success, that you teach me that there is a path where it is important to dream.

I challenge, that you complement my life, that you teach me, that every moment I must fight.

Challenge, owner of the present, owner of time, owner of reality.

Challenge, that you enrich my soul, you enrich my spirit, you enrich my experience.

Challenge, that in each challenge you give me more energy, more strength, more life.

When the challenges appeared in my life, my knowledge grew, I knew wisdom.

Challenge, you made me compete with my being, my inner strength.

Challenge, he taught me that progress requires decision, courage and courage.

I was filled with challenges that gave meaning to my life, I knew love.

Challenge, you come to my life, like water in the desert, like food in the famine.

The challenges I have in my life, they build me, they teach me that my present is constant struggle.

I challenge, that you activate my mind, that you fill me with energy, that you activate me for action.

I challenge, you complement my life, interesting my day, because it has significant challenges.

Challenge, charismatic, that gives me motivation to continue my path to success.

Challenge, the signal of intensity, the signal of full bliss, the sign of optimism.

Challenge, I teach that creativity comes when the challenge is challenging.

Challenge, it is life, it is love, it is the greatest road that leads to the spiritual universe.

Without challenges life has no riches, experiences do not arrive, the existential vacuum appears.

Challenge, introduce yourself to my life, so that it is occupied with genius, to act every moment.

Challenge, teach me that my life makes sense, that I am an active constructor of my present.

Challenge, create in my experience, so that my legacy is infinite.

Challenge, teach me to build the world, beginning to build my interior.

May the next challenge, fill me with enjoyment, enjoyment, fill me with happiness.

Challenge, that when enjoying my joy rises, when doing my work with the maximum effort.

Challenge, restlessness touched my door, taught me that the wealth of options, forget the stormy past.

Challenge, complement of existence, competition fills my stage with virtues.

Challenge, awards, medals, glory, is the satisfaction of total delivery day by day.

Challenge, you came to my life when I least expected it, when I thought I was lost.

Challenge, which made me active, gave me energy, I came back to believe that dreams come true.

Challenge, is what I want, the challenge that made me be born again.

Challenge, that made me grow inside, creating an active path of genius.

I challenge, simply the great challenges in my present, in my life, in my heart.

Competitors fill their lives with challenges, so that their hearts beat hard, so that they know, that their life in this world is for something, when your life is full of challenges, you lose the notion of time, it is enriched every moment, struggles every day making the most effort, you do not look for a prize, you simply look for having given all your strength to the challenge that was presented to you, your reward was to feel more alive, fill yourself with challenges in your path, so that the fabulous experience that will come your way will arrive teaching you, that your life has meaning and that your legacy will be effective for future generations, that in your grave is written the word never, never gave up, thank you very much teacher for his words, for the great philosophy that he transmits.

Competitors, in these small cars that you see, are solar powered, we will transport you to the lake where we will swim the first test that is 1,500 meters., After we leave the lake and make the transition in the bicycles that will be in front of us, each bicycle has your name of each of you, will be 40 kilometers hard, on a special road that meets the distance, then we leave the bicycles and continue running the 10 kilometers, which will be the final test, the goal will be waiting for us an earthly paradise, You will see it when they complete the whole journey, all of us who make the journey, we will go to the sound of the shot, our meeting point will be at the finish, all the signs are sophisticated, they will have a memory of the race, so that when they like they can to be observed in the challenge, competitors to approach the cars, each one has his name, I see them in the exit.

What a great challenge, I am really amazed at what we are going to do, I know that I am not a competitor, but with all the training I have led, the union with the competitors, I feel part of them, it will be a great challenge, we arrived with the solar cars to the place of departure, we expect a beautiful lake, the water is crystal clear, turquoise blue, we breathe a unique air combined with nature, that beautiful scenery, the teachers observe all the competitors, young we are at the point of meeting of exit, the judges observe us, they will have special monitors where they will observe all the competition, good competitors the minutes pass in 2 minutes we will begin the great challenge, in their marks, the shot sounds, infinity of helicopters fly around us, we We enter the water, we all have a special energy, we are all hungry for success, we all do the test at a similar pace, but some begin to get ahead, the teachers they are participating, then we have no pretexts for the great challenges, teachers enjoy exercising, participate in competitions, some are getting ahead, but my condition grows, almost all of us go out equal, in the 1,500 meters of the lake, I feel like heart beats with strength, as if it wanted to burst or get out of place, but it is great, the human body, as our body is the most wonderful machine in the world, God created us to do what we propose in life.

I go running I read my name on the Richc bike, each one picks up his two-wheeled vehicle, the big challenge begins, the climbs and descents, I never imagined it was so great to take a tour with professional bicycles, the one I bring is light, like the wind, I go so fast that I forget the fatigue, I observe the splendorous landscape, we walk a special track, for our bicycles, there are very steep climbs, I use the changes is great, as technology gives you power, we indicate the signs that we are going kilometer 21, we take a little more than half, we almost reached 40 kilometers, in fact the landscape is so wonderful, the air enters my lungs filling my body with energy, sweat bathes my whole body, fatigue begins to feel, but I must continue with force, I know that this challenge, will make me grow very much mentally, physically, ideologically, it is a privilege to know my body, to know that I can perform extraordinary things, my body adapted to the great effort, my heart has already adapted, my body knows that it is something great that is living, it is pain, with maximum enjoyment at the same time, I feel alive, all my senses are awake enjoying from this great moment, we are at kilometer 32, the climbs are more complicated, but this great bike helps me too much, is aware of the effort made, we feel a single body, and the bicycle is part of my body, we are one, the competitors do not give up, they continue the road, the great road to realization, as this track is designed for a great competition, any athlete would like to be in this great scenario, we are privileged, we are enjoying the best of the world, in the best scenario in the world, with the best people in the world, 2 kilometers to complete the second stage and know that we still have to run the last 10 kilometers, I'm going to program my mind, I'll imagine, I'm starting, the pain has to be in the past, I have to live in the moment, I own this moment, I own this time lapse, 1 kilometer is almost finished, the hydrating drink is great as it makes my whole body feel fresh, my cells are so hydrated, they can not imagine the great effort that I am making, these last few meters feel a bit far away, we are all doing our best, all the philosophy that we have received It has been great for our training, the whole philosophy is focused on the efforts, challenges, obstacles that come our way in life, it's great, like the philosophies we've heard, every time we analyze them we talk about reality what it happens around us, we are champions and we are demonstrating it, we do not know who will be the winner, we all have the same profile, the same need that is to succeed, now if we fulfill the 40 kilometers in bicycles

We leave our vehicles parked, we change tennis, we are all sure fast of what we are doing, it is great as the group goes evenly in the transitions, all have desires to win, the race will give us the spiritual effectiveness of achieving the maximum effort, it is complicated know who will be the winner, but we will all be successful, to run, the teachers almost reach us is very little difference, they have a lot of condition, they thought it would be easy to beat us, but I know we have a need for particular triumph, it will be a hard way, my legs feel faint, but at the same time, my mind motivates them to continue, I'm resting from the bike I think, that is the only test I'm doing, I hope my body understands that I need more energy, I never imagined being so good athlete, I know that the mind takes you to unexplored places, a path that has never been traveled, it's wonderful, we're all almost on the same level, but these climbs are deadly, some are ahead, others reach, we take an extreme step in which nobody wants to give up their place, but the faint is great, but our spirit gives us strength, who knows where.

Kilometer 3, I'm getting tired but they are great these moments, they teach me that we have extraordinary abilities, that only come to light in times of crisis, there is a lot of knowledge that we do not know, that's why we occupy a very low percentage of our extraordinary capacities, Today on this day I realize that our body is so great and wonderful, that each day gives us a new learning, even learning is observed more in the challenges, kilometer 5 the landscapes are great, I focus on them, I feel their smell, their images are reflected, I catch their sounds, of the falling waterfalls, the sound of the animals, whisper my ears, that make me amaze, that I am in a place I never imagined, kilometer 6 and almost, the teachers reach us It can not be where they get so much strength, we increase our pace, we will not let them win, we increase the pace, we are motivated, it is a special force that we do not know where it came from, I turn to see the face of the teachers, they are amazed they thought that they would win us easily, they are seeing that we are all strong and we have the desire to succeed at any cost.

kilometer 7, there are some participants who are lagging behind, I want to give up, let everyone pass me, enjoy the great prize that is rest, but not everything that has been done so far has been great, I can not give it's great to think about resting, but it's better to meet the goal and then enjoy the great rest, kilometer 8, we all accelerate, but my legs do not give me more, what I do, two kilometers are missing, the heaviest from all the competition, it's great to compete, I feel alive, it's fabulous to feel that there is little left to achieve the goal, the teachers accelerate, it's great we all try to do the same, but our bodies do not respond, we all know that the efforts do not end, that the only rest is in the cemetery, we have to work to the maximum, in the face of adversity, in the face of exhaustion, before what is presented, my best reward will be when the competition ends.

They are exceeding me, we are almost reaching kilometer 9 I can see it, I am going to try harder, it is only 1 kilometer, I reach all, the teachers are amazed that I reach them, we all accelerate the pace, we know that it is the end, only 600 meters missing, the teacher accelerates to the maximum the teacher is staying behind, I am losing sight of the teacher, will be the winner, the teacher accelerates, but it is difficult to achieve, I can not continue, I demand more to my legs but they do not want to continue, they overwhelm me I do not know how many, I close my eyes, I forget the result, I am happy that I almost reach my goal, I am reaching a great phenomenal stadium, I recover energy, I am 400 meters away. , there are two competitors that go ahead of me, even if I die I am going to pass them, there is no stomach, it starts acting very strange, I win them by half a step, they also decided to give their last effort to the maximum, cross the finish line once, e stoy being born again, my way is my heart, grateful for the great rest, several people approaching asking me if I'm okay, if I tell them I feel sensational, wonderful, fantastic, thank you, but it's something unique, the competitors keep coming, you can see them a great happiness to have fulfilled the goal that we all feel that we earn too much. After 40 minutes a strong voice is heard, competitors, I have the list of winners, all have been winners, but we will mention, as they were arriving, to receive a commemorative medal to the first, second, third place in the women's branch and manly, the places they stayed like this;

LADIES:

1.- Professor Yessica

2.- Rosalinda

3.- Giselle

4.- Queenie

5.- Joharim

6.- Florecet

7.- Akeilas

GENTLEMEN

1.- Professor Salomomr

2.- Ryud

3.- Mahatmae

4.- Richc

5.- Jenst

6.- Winstond

7.- Joao

These are the great places, no matter what place they got, they were champions, they fulfilled a great class, they fulfilled themselves, they transcended in this life making their best effort, they are all winners, they receive this great sincere applause, receive these words I hope they reach your heart, says so;

Champion

You have fought day by day, between storms.

Fatigue has not stopped you, courage has strengthened you.

When alternatives no longer existed, they continued to look for options in the evening.

You never had notion of time, your priority was to work to the maximum without waiting for any prize.

Your mentality grew, each time a new challenge presented itself.

You have believed in the great miracle that dreams come true, with discipline and dedication.

You know that miracles exist, that they come many times when we feel lost.

I fell many times, I got up again, continue my way.

Fight tirelessly, cry countless times, not finding a solution.

I cried countless times, for not finding an exit, for not obtaining the minimum result.

The universe witnessed my effort, my understanding of never giving up.

I was bored with only seeing darkness, I could not find the light.

My work did not pay off, I felt anger that my effort did not work, I fought harder.

I got used to defeat, I asked heaven, because the minimum result did not come.

I cried again in a bitter way, I became more spiritual, I asked for better results with my heart.

I promised that, if I saw the light, I would be grateful forever, believing forever that miracles exist.

My tiredness wanted to defeat me, but it was the opposite, I felt stronger.

I began to enjoy what I was doing, I fell in love with my days, fatigue disappeared.

I started to see a small bright light, I thought it was not reality.

I saw the first result was great, it is minimal, but I saw it as a great achievement.

Fate is a great adversary, which must be faced with courage and courage.

Day by day, we deal with personal battles, these contests are the hardest.

I was creating a necessary profile, to fight to live, with intensity and love.

My crises have taken me to the ground, the wounds have wanted to stop me, but I get up.

I know that constant motivation will make powerful things happen.

I became authentic, I thought it was a mistake, but the present showed me its strength.

I always found in my mind to fight to be better than yesterday.

Living today to the fullest taught me, that I have no other opportunity, nothing else that presents itself.

I'm going to do everything on my part to get positive results.

The fear disappeared, emerged acting with courage in life, in love, on the road to success.

Our ancestors did more dangerous things, to survive, even dying fighting.

Today what we see as a challenge, maybe it is not.

We have many tools to achieve our goals, even technology is on our side.

I am a warrior who faces risks, conquers pain, builds dreams.

Today they call me champion, they only see my victories, they do not observe the path of storms that happens.

In historical times you fought for everything, today you just have to fight to live to the fullest.

I feel motivated to continue fighting and achieve more, I know that it is possible, I have the experience that the pain has left me.

Champion, I am full of scars, when the enjoyment comes I do it with energy, I enjoy it to the fullest.

Champion, my prize is the joy of never quitting fighting, of never giving up, that the scenario that presents itself to me is something new.

My challenges, my challenges, I take them as something new, a place where I should try my best, it's a new day.

Champion, I fell, I failed, I woke up, I knew the top, I fell back, I am a warrior willing to face whatever comes up.

I have come from nowhere, I am a miracle of life, my constant achievements are miracles, that many times I imagine I am dreaming.

I made many sacrifices, which did not affect me, they gave me a great philosophy of life, which is in my present.

Champion, every day is a new one, I must be fit, for the next challenge, the next battle.

Champion, rather I am a warrior ready to face, what comes my way today.

Champion, the notion of time has disappeared, because every day I live it to the fullest.

I enjoy the things that many call simple, they are the basis of my sense of life.

Champion, my work is a legacy to motivate future generations to have a better world.

Champion, feedback is important, listening to the great heroes of history, fills me with wealth.

Champion, I never imagined this word, my days of constant struggle, were filled with simple trophies, which for me were forever valuable.

Champion my life is full of joy and happiness.

Champion my spirit grows day by day.

Champion, only the universe is witness, I am only better today in this present, than I was yesterday.

What great words, exactly reach the heart, transport us, teach us the real philosophy of life, even the great leaders of all history, show us that, during his life, he was full of sacrifices, that to get where they are, they had to fight tirelessly, how wonderful is all this.

Competitors, will be transported to a special place, where we will consent, where you will see how important it is to enjoy a prize, keep fighting for your goals, every day is a new day, I am your friend Professor Teslac, enjoy as much as possible who comes they deserve it.

They transport us in all terrain solar cars, how great they use technology for development, improving the quality of the air, we climbed, we went through a great place where there are crops of all fruits and vegetables, I never imagined that the food that exists in This place is cultivated, I even read, that this place is a sustainable place, that even all agriculture is organic, what is left is exported, for all, the staff that make up the group of the 10 richest people in the world, they have with countless companies where their staff, they are given the best, they have a great diet, they are like their children, they say they are a great global family, we are reaching a majestic fortress, everything is white, bright, highlights before the immense sun, it is a great jewel surrounded by this wonderful place.

We arrive to indicate us, that we are going to receive a massage, they introduce us to a great room, that counts with infinity of great apparatuses, with the objetivó to rehabilitate our bodies, after receiving a reward so rewarding, we were in the sauna, in great vats whirlpool, we enjoyed a great meal, the chefs took pains to satisfy our palates, it is great to be in this place, enjoying the great prize, the music penetrates all the senses, the smell is relaxing, I feel in paradise, know what a few moments ago I was suffering to arrive and achieve my long-awaited goal, to finish the competition test, if we compare everything we do in life, no matter how much effort we make, it will give us a reward, that even if it is minimal, we can even breathe more quiet gives us a full bliss, relaxation gives us strength, to continue our path to success, after great enjoyment, teachers tell us that in 10 minutes, we They wait in the room winners, to give us the last indications, it feels sad to stop enjoying, but the road has to continue, it is well said that the success of yesterday , we have to continue our way, looking for new challenges, new goals, new goals, for when the great time of enjoyment comes we will also do it with great joy, the great motivation is when you achieve the desired goal, it gives you strength and encouragement to continue continuing.

We arrived at the great hall triumphant, infinity of photos of the greatest leaders of the history they fill the place, that great honor to its name, is a great semblance of all the great histories of life, where we have the facility to take the things more important, the philosophies that led them to succeed, the professors are in the center of the room, surrounded by trophies, recognition, all triumph that has given an antecedent, the teacher speaks, it is my privilege to give them my greatest recognition, tell As always, I admire them, they are a great group, they have given me a lot of knowledge, strength, philosophy that we can achieve what we want, today was a lot of learning, this competition felt like it was the first, I received a special lesson, that there is no weak competitor, on the contrary there are competitors that give you great surprises, observe his face of tireless struggle, the thirst to succeed, his eyes shone with inte nsidad, their bodies were willing to make the efforts that were necessary to achieve their goals, it was a great learning, it was a great competition.

I leave you with your teacher Yessica, competitors, as the professor says, I am also amazed by his great dedication, by the superhuman efforts they made, we are elite athletes, we have been competing for many years, he has left us great experiences, they make known the profile of the great athletes, today they showed their great abilities, I know that several are amazed by their great participation, their great motivation led them to successfully complete the big test, the body is a wonderful machine, unique, difficult to understand, but that takes us to incredible places worthy of a miracle, the universe is witness to our great dedication, our great desires to achieve our dreams, today I observe a very united team, all with the same mentality, with the same spiritual sense, they are warriors, because they gave their souls in this great battle, they are all winners, because today they learned something fantastic, their c wonderful bodies is an amazing machine that we did not finish knowing, that leaves us amazed of its great capacities, God created our bodies in a magnificent way, so that every day we would be amazed by the great natural tools that we have for our human development, I congratulate competitors, they are a great team, I am proud to belong to this great project, they are great people who, as the teacher said, give us feedback, we have finished this great day, we hope they will be renewed with a greater force that characterizes them.

What philosophy my God, I feel that this place is one of the most important in my life, the learning that I am getting is unique and incomparable, I am going to fulfill almost two months in this great place and my amazement is not lost, every day is a new day full of knowledge and wisdom, we went to our last class Yoga Bioenergetics II, it is 5:50 pm we are in the great stadium that sees us being born every time we are here, we are in the classroom, Professor Noetherli, as is always at the center, welcome competitors I know you have had a wonderful day, everyone in a relaxing position, said a great sage is important to die to live, what meaning do these words have, when you enjoy everything around you as if you were going to die, when you do all things as if you were no longer being, when you love with great force as if you were going to die, your life is filled with special karma, a field of light surrounds you that you are aware exists, but there are people who they observe it, that field of force, always gives you light before the storms, before the great darkness, life smiles at you, you have to live, you feel alive, you give special value to your body and your spirit.

Guys, let's get energized, let's start our rehabilitation class, let's make yoga part of our lives, with gratitude and love the universe will witness our coordination with all our cardinal points, after the great positions of energetic yoga, we are all born again With more energy, competitors I wish the best for you, in this room you breathe a natural environment where the combination of energy is the priority, always relax, breathe in a way that you feel your inhalation with energy, feel how your body is revitalized, they are filled with strength, feel alive, enjoy life to the fullest, only live once, ask for the best in life, meet with people who have their type of energy, who are positive, who are constructive, so that together achieve a better world, when you change inwardly, the results observe you around you, the magnificent energies surround your heart, your sen sibility awakens, your emotions are born directed towards a single objective, give priority to happiness and love, when you love with strength without expecting what you receive, you feel a great satisfaction, that the result does not depend on you, you gave yourself maximum to love, the universe is a witness of your great offering, you live life to the fullest, that is to live, it is to be alive.

Competitors rest, enjoy their great moments, dream that when you least expect it, comes the great miracle that makes dreams come true, rest recover, fight to the fullest, they are the best, they are a great group, they have great projects that will benefit many lives around of the world. What great comments of the teacher, is real knowledge, is maximum wisdom, is the reality of life was a great day, to write it in a great life story.

Today is the month is Saturday, at 3 o'clock in the afternoon we will know who is the next competitor who is retiring, these moments are difficult, nobody wants to leave, nobody wants to stop enjoying these great moments, everything here is great, it is the dream come true of any leader in the world, have a wonderful place where you receive unique knowledge that strengthens your personality, your self-esteem, self-realization, the most important treasure that is wisdom, treat us like kings, is something that most that is in this place we have not received, that treatment that they give us, offers us a lot of energy to work and stay firm in this great place, at 3:00 p.m., the teachers will tell us who is the next one to leave, all the competitors are thoughtful for this great day, nobody wants to leave, but everyone knows that there will be only one winner, that I would say that since we are in this great place, enjoying what surrounds us, the magnificent the deals that they give us, we are already winners.

We enter the great hall, all the professors are on the big podium, in front of us, watching us, I know they want nobody to leave, but they know of the great responsibility that the great winner will have, competitors I am his teacher McYuretzili, I have the great I work to dismiss the next competitor, I have the honor to comment on behalf of all the teachers present here, which for us is a great job that lasts 3 days to this day, that with the exhaustive analysis that we do, according to the results we know which will be the next competitor that retires from this great competition, we know that during our careers in life, we have many obstacles that are productive because they fill us with experience, when our life presents challenges, our path becomes bigger, our life is enriched by unique experiences, your journey in this place has been magnificent, you have left your sweat, your tears, your abilities and n each test, in each challenge that is presented to us, it is very difficult for us when this moment comes to decide who is the one who is retiring, it costs us a lot of work, since everyone is qualified for this great test, they all show it in his total commitment, in his strength at every moment to achieve his goals.

The person who is going to leave this great and beautiful place is, a fighter who always made his maximum effort, that out there life will present him with infinite opportunities, that due to his abilities, he will take advantage of them, the person who retires, is a great leader, who worked hard every day, knew what awaited him, knew he had a great responsibility that is not over, the world is waiting for him to transmit what he knows, his great knowledge, his great potential, competitor who is leaving;

10.-Name: Jenst

   Age: 31 years

   Country: Denmark

   Profession: PhD in philosophy

   Project: build happiness

   Sport: Rugby

   Language: Danish, English.

   Altruism for the world: It has been found that happiness is a global need, specific objective to make organizations around the world dedicated to happiness.

The name and the data were heard with resignation, but with energetic applause, having fulfilled and developed with all their effort, their warrior personality, the tears overflow in the place, it is a great farewell, the teacher continues, she loses a great competitor, but there are 10 willing to give their best, goodbye hurts, but often the big constructions, require great sacrifices, to achieve the dreams are due to be sacrifices, many times until the future is appreciated the great work, what if I invite you to keep fighting to be better, to use your tools with maximum effort, have the help of us their teachers, who are willing to deliver at all times the best we have for their development, for that this great Mission project, eliminate world poverty, transcend in all times, where history is witness that all available forces were delivered, all a positive mentality, total dedication, all the necessary efforts to achieve the great goal.

We dismiss the competitor Jents with enthusiasm and love, it is a great farewell where emotions come together between sadness, joy, illusions, retreat through a tunnel full of light, competitors continue forward with their projects, continue to strive, with the premise of being better every day, today is the most important day of my life, at this moment is when I'm going to try my best, forgetting about time, only thinking about the benefit I will give to humanity in the world, all their projects are great, visualize yourself as winners, show why you are here, surprise with your ideas, rest, save energy for the great moments that await you, count on our support to the fullest, we are part of a great project that will go down in history, retreat with the face up, dream of your project, miracles exist, have a great day.

We all retired, two emotions bring us a bit of sadness and at the same time the happiness of not being selected to go out, the competitors, will rest relaxed today knowing that Monday is a great day of competition, I go to my house to observe the monitors This is the last time the great guru speaks with Jents. The great moment arrives I see it on the monitor, great guru I am here again, but today I feel sad, desolate, defeated, I feel a lump in my throat, unburden yourself son, I know what you are going through, it is something incredible to accept, you go of a great place, but the world that needs your contribution awaits you, you need to transmit your new personality, your new knowledge, your new way of seeing life, to teach everyone that you are alive and that you accept the challenge of doing things extraordinary, that complement your life, that make you transcend, great guru, thank you for your great words, give me a big breath, let me know why I was here.

If son hurt the farewells, there is a special duel, for anything we lose, the important thing is to express our feelings, have the courage to accept our condition and keep fighting, to know that the world gives us many opportunities, you lose a battle, but the continuous war, you are a great warrior who must be prepared for the next contest, take all the good things that I give you this great place, all the dreams that you manifested being here, all the creativity that arose in you, all the learning, all the knowledge that they gave you, more tools to continue your journey, feel your loss, value your way, value every moment, be grateful with life, be grateful with everything you receive, however small it may be, that will give you an abundance profile that you will share during your life, your knowledge is valuable, when I leave here I know that you will share it, because you are interested in human development, you are a great human being of great feeling s, take advantage of all the options that are presented to you, your life continues, all the great past you've had, take it as a great experience, dream of countless situations that will make you a builder.

I know that when you leave here, you will always look for the most precious thing that is happiness for you, enjoy what you do, enjoy love to the fullest, continue to build your great personality, remember that you are a unique person in this life, you will agree with countless mentalities, you will have some traits that compare you with someone, but in the end all the inhabitants of the world are different, each individual is unique, enjoy your strengths, learn from your weaknesses, circulate your world with courage, thank you great guru, They seal their goodbye with a big hug, Jents retires, it was a great privilege to have your presence.

CHAPTER V

It is Sunday morning classes begin again, today is a day to relax and analyze these two great months that have passed, It is relevant to know how time passes so fast, but in all our goals is the transcendence of being here dreaming in this great place, a place of great wealth, which is tattooed on our skins in a magnificent way, the project is a single union, a single body, a single soul, you know the great responsibility, but at the same time, the great challenge that is be here, the subjects that we will take are the following ones;

Monday	Teacher	Subject
8:00 to 10:45	Salomomr	Physical and mental training III
11:00 to 12:45	Laeva	Global Leadership III
12:50 to 13:50	FOOD	
14:00 to 15:45	Teslac	Innovation III
16:00 to 17:45	McYuretzili	Communication and understanding III
18:00 to 18:55	Edisonic	Transcendental Ideas III
19:00 to 20:00	Noetherli	Yoga Bioenergetics III

Tuesday	Teacher	Subject

8:00 to 10:45	Salomomr	Sports Philosophy and Training III
11:00 to 12:45	Markl	Human Development III
12:50 to 13:50	FOOD	
14:00 to 15:45	Vincir	Creatividad III
16:00 to 17:45	Curielm	Motivation III
18:00 to 18:55	Yessica	Positive Mentality III
19:00 to 20:00	Noetherli	Yoga Bioenergetics III

Wednesday	**Teacher**	**Subject**
8:00 to 10:45	Yessica	Training special forces III
11:00 to 12:45	Laeva	Global Leadership III
12:50 to 13:50	FOOD	
14:00 to 15:45	Teslac	Innovation III
16:00 to 17:45	McYuretzili	Communication and understanding III
18:00 to 18:55	Edisonic	Transcendental Ideas III
19:00 to 20:00	Noetherli	Yoga Bioenergetics III

Thursday	**Teacher**	**Subject**

8:00 to 10:45   Salomomr Sports Philosophy and Training III

11:00 to 12:45   Markl   Human Development III

12:50 to 13:50   FOOD

14:00 to 15:45   Vincir   Creatividad III

16:00 to 17:45   Curielm   Motivation III

18:00 to 18:55   Yessica   Positive Mentality III

19:00 to 20:00   Noetherli   Yoga Bioenergetics III

Friday	**Teacher**	**Subject**
8:00 to 10:45 III	Salomomr	Physical and mental training III
11:00 to 12:45	Markl	Communication III
12:50 to 13:50	FOOD	
14:00 to 15:45	Vincir	Creatividad III
16:00 to 17:45	Curielm	Motivation III
18:00 to 18:55	Yessica	Positive Mentality III
19:00 to 20:00	Noetherli	Yoga Bioenergetics III

Saturday	**Teacher**	**Subject**

8:00 to 17:45 Salomomr Training Exploration Forces

Yessica Specials III

18:00 to 20:00   Noetherli   Yoga Bioenergetics III

Sunday

Strategic rest; with work options according to the needs of the participant.

Important note:

All the subjects are focused, with the project of each competitor.

We continue with the great learning, we all have the great culture of maximum effort, the classes are great, each competitor develops his project better, the exchange of ideas of wealth and learning, the development of each student is magnificent, each one encourages the participation, all have a special interest in knowledge, we breathe in such a great atmosphere that the feedback is splendid, the third week comes again, the teachers have used this day as the greatest challenge, which awaits us, to enjoy these great moments of unique development; the professors wait for us to give us the surprise of what will happen, says Professor Yessica, competitors as we are always willing to give the maximum effort, their initiative must be fleeting, for any challenge that comes their way, they are great leaders, that day with day they have to demonstrate that this facts, the proof is the following, an air force ship will lead us as great warriors to the track that is near the beach where the test will be the following:

We will swim from the edge of the beach in deep water to the infinite island, they are five kilometers away, they have already been measured according to their accuracy, they will have special signals, which will give them visibility towards the objective, upon reaching the shore of the island, they will see the goal announcement, they will cross it after they leave the seashore, running are 200mts. Spectacular travel, will have a bracelet, where there will be people to analyze their trajectories, their health, their vital signs, if they see any deterioration, they will immediately remove them from the water, there will be solar energy boats to remove them from the competition.

Listening to all the indications, we are ready for the great test, the great challenge. The teacher is with you, maybe life has many surprises, this is a battlefield where extraordinary battles are expected, nobody is obliged to comply with them, whoever wishes can give up, retire and appear in the next class , raise your hand if you want to go, there is the jet that will take you back to the comfort zone, the teacher waits in silence, no one raises your hand, thank you competitors, they are mine, I know they accept the great challenge , this is not a pool, they will be in the maximum stage that is the natural, the sea will receive them with their power, close our eyes we will make a great prayer so that the great stage allows our entrance, we have the greatest security in the world, but If the sea does not accept our entrance to their domains it will be more complicated, close your eyes listen and repeat with me mentally the prayer.

Great Sea

Today, this day we make the decision to explore your body.

We ask for your permission to be in your great place, in your territory.

We do not know what awaits us, I ask you to protect us from all the negative.

We feel fear, but if you make things easier for us, you will give us great courage.

We humbly ask you, take our journey, feel your strength, while allowing you to explore.

Our prayer is from the heart, we want to know you and at the same time continue our path to success.

We know about your power, we know about your greatness, we know that we still have a lot to know.

Bless our way, it is to transcend, if you did not allow it, we have the courage to follow our path.

If you allow it, we will be grateful forever.

The universe is witness to our fulfillment, that the challenges that are presented we receive them with determination and love.

Great sea today we decided to explore you, with all the respect you deserve.

Great sea, we made the decision to meet you, to feel you, to smell you, to try you sometimes.

Great sea, we will continue our way, to transcend in the history of our life.

Great sea, feel our hearts as they beat with force, how they live to the fullest.

Great sea, great sea, great sea.

Open your eyes slowly, ready competitors to make the great effort, in 5 minutes will announce the exit, what a great test, my God, I am very afraid, the adrenaline runs through my body, but at the same time I have the courage to want to know the unknown , there are 5 minutes in which all the faces are scared to face the great challenge, a strong voice is heard, competitors ready, a shot sounds that resounds in the sky, we begin, it is difficult to test I feel very afraid, it is not like a pool , is to face the unknown, my body is rocked, right, left, the waves collide with my body, I am reassuring myself and that I must do, if my heart rate does not increase and they take me out of this place, I am already assimilating the great challenge , the good thing that the tools that provide us are so great and futuristic, I perfectly observe my way, it is great, I observe as with my natural sight, I imagine that these lenses would not let me observe my path, never imagine being in this place, help me, my God, I know that I am prepared for this and the teachers also know it, otherwise they would not encourage these tests.

We all go in a group, it's great, we all have the same intensity, the same enthusiasm, the same strength, the test is great, I realize this day, there is no easy challenge, everything in this life has its degree of difficulty, Anyway, it is important when you perform the challenge, enjoy the great find, enjoy the great achievement, I realize that it is different to swim in a pool, to swim in the sea, there is an infinity of flora and fauna, which is observed in our course, I observe the goal, it is close, but at the same time we see that we do not advance, I feel a special challenge, I am already enjoying this great moment, I feel the power of the sun, as it penetrates my body, it is a great natural state, a boat is coming out Joao, if I understand I also wanted to give up, I guess he never wanted to give up, was the monitoring they are doing their vital signs, also the waves have increased, oh also They're taking Florencet out.

We all observe but we continue our journey in a single group and the test is difficult, but in life that is easy, we have to fight with courage, we do not know what comes to us when we fight to achieve our goals, we are warriors, willing to deliver the best of us, after a long lapse of time, we are reaching the finish line, one kilometer left, I will win, I will try my best, it has to be my great victory, but it is difficult, it seems that the others listen to my thoughts, we think in the same way we are one, a great group great, you feel the effort of the whole group, but there are some who are swimming more powerful, it does not make him die but I will win, I will keep fighting until the end, I and the teacher are arriving at the same time, when leaving the beach and running the last 200 meters, I fell, I could not keep the balance, I reached the goal failing, I hydrated as much as I can consume all the fruits that that they provide us, the places of competence were as follows;

Ladies

1.- Professor Yessica

2.- Rosalinda

3.- Queenie

4.- Giselle

5.- Joharim

6.- Akeilas

GENTLEMEN

1.- Professor Salomomr

2.- Richc

3.- Mahatmae

4.- Ryud

5.- Winstond

What a great competition, it's a big dream I can not believe I get second and I almost beat the teacher, I can not believe this great miracle is great, I feel super happy to have finished this great challenge, I will go to the next podium from my great teacher, Professor Yessica won again, they are great athletes, worthy of a great example. Competitors congratulations, for fulfilling this great goal, it was great to see how they made an effort, we know that everyone has great abilities, even those who had to retire in the competition.

Florecet and Joao, we all congratulate you, we give you our highest recognition, we mentioned the difficult part of the test that we were about to give up, not to continue, but we were able to control our vital signs, which gave us the power to continue, competitors feel happy about the achievement since they entered the great sea and were champions, is a great challenge that makes them special, we will take them to a special place where they enjoyed the great achievement, as they received the respective medals of the first 3 places we retired in a few cars land, with solar technology, after 25 minutes of travel, we arrive at the great structure that awaits our arrival, it is a futuristic gold construction, our bodies reach an aromatic air that reaches 360 degrees of our body.

It is a place like all that we have been fantastic, you can see from this place the majestic island, it is surprising, the great vegetation, the great fauna, the great structures that surround them, but this place is great in the four points there are amazing landscapes , we are going to eat we get on the elevator we are on the last floor a revolving restaurant awaits us, the person who introduces us to the place, presses a keyboard, all the glass around us disappears, we are in a natural place, in a unique place, We eat great, it is important to celebrate the great find in this way, since we finished eating we are transported to a large room, where the smell is relaxing, the music is great, I feel in a special place, I use the touch screen I program to wake me up in 1 hour, I'm exhausted, I'm going to relax, the seat is great, too relaxing, very modern, I watch the screen where it tells me the way I want to enjoy it.

After we rest, they tell us to go to the massage area, it's great to want to stay in this place, relax one too, recover my energy, I'm happy of my great participation in this competition, all have been fabulous, but this was great because almost won, we are in the sauna area, after that we take a bath, again to rest, as they allow us, after the great hell of competition, comes the calm, the enjoyment, the great enjoyment, the teachers tell us to rest , in 1 hour I see them in the magnifiquert room, turn on their alarm clocks set them 10 minutes before, this place is great as they allow us, it's great, when you try hard and the prize even if the rest is great.

The alarm sounds it's time to get up, it's great to rest, it's a great prize, I'm going to the meeting point to the magnifiquert room, we all arrive punctually, the teachers are in the great room, Professor Yessica speaks, competitors today was a great day we fulfilled a great goal, the competitors that had to leave, I know that deep down they wanted to continue, but there are times that the goals must be postponed, so that in the next participation it will be with greater intensity, decision, during the life, the important is to try, find the objectives with the greatest interest, always giving the greatest effort, if the result is not given, we will have several opportunities in our life, to continue fighting, on our way to success there will be several options, we will take advantage of them, it was a great test, difficult, we all know that swimming in a pool is safer, than a place created by our magnificent nature, our fulfillment is perfect, we are conscious If our life will be full of challenges forever, our path to success will not be easy, it will be complicated, many times we will wish not to continue, but the great strength, the great spirit will motivate us to continue, then the teacher will speak to them;

The great roads of life

Life is great, it shows us a path of several options.

It is important to experiment, to find the right side, the side that makes us enjoy what we do.

A life without challenges is not fun, it lacks emotion, meaning, love.

Greatness is not measured by a single activity, it is measured by a total personality.

There are easy roads where anyone can travel.

On difficult, sophisticated, special, unique roads, where only the champions live.

In the course of life a fleeting mentality teaches you, the sketch to success.

The stars look distant, but the spirit has ways to reach them.

The positive mentality creates paths of light, security, understanding.

The great paths of life are full of unforgettable experiences.

It is my priority to manifest the great work, discipline, to build the foundations of success.

I do not want material things, I always ask for the greatness of wisdom.

The great paths of life are a treasure that is important to remember forever.

Your path has been difficult, but in this life nothing is easy.

Your interest in achieving what you propose, makes your life interesting, unique.

The great roads of life are great to live, look for them with enthusiasm.

Failures will stop you, however difficult your priority is to get up, continue your way, nothing has happened.

The obstacles have given you energy, experience, challenges that have given you strengths.

The great paths of life, I have been surprised by the great experience of living them.

To get to them, I've been through storms, obscurities, I've had to dare.

Courage has been my priority, fear had to bury him on the road.

The great paths of life have taught me that life is great, it is magnificent.

My life is interesting because it is full of challenges.

My life is interesting, because I own every moment, for that reason I try my best.

The great paths of life are the great path I want in my life.

The great paths of life are the reward for maximum effort.

The great paths of life are happiness and love.

Great competitors continue their great path to success, many battles await them, it gave me great pleasure to belong today to a great team, where spirituality, love and transcendence is the fundamental, I congratulate you and thank you very much for your great participation, it's great for me and the teacher, to be part of a great team.

It is great to receive so much philosophy of life, it is great to receive so many words of encouragement, there are no pretexts to stop continuing our journey, teachers teach us with enthusiasm and determination the essential, wonderful ways of life.

It has been very rewarding, tomorrow is 3 months of being in this great place, tomorrow another competitor is removed, I do not know who will be, but all competitors have to be thoughtful, everyone thinks the same way, they can be the next participant It's been extraordinary days, I'm going to rest tomorrow at 3 o'clock in the afternoon and we'll know who is leaving. The next day is 14:50, we are all anxious, impatient, who will be the next eliminated participant no one wants to leave.

With you, Professor Markl, we are gathered in this wonderful day, to attest to the next eliminated participant, it was 3 great days where all the teachers, added to this project a great support, it was difficult like all competition, but we have a lot of responsibility under from our shoulders, it is important to do everything in the best way, all of you are great competitors, how time passes, the selection is more difficult, everyone gets great grades, but we know the great responsibility of getting an absolute winner, the next competitor who retires from this great competition is a great person like all worthy of recognition, remember that the twelve participants were selected in a very sophisticated way that makes them the best in the world, the great competitor that retires is;

1.- Name: Florencet

   Age: 28 years

   Country: Canada

   Profession: Geological Engineer

   Project: Drinking water for everyone

   Sport: Gymnast

   Language: English and French

   Altruism for the world: Through pure water to fulfill the primordial need.

It is very hard to receive the news of the one who leaves, but at the same time I observe among the competitors, the respite of relief at not being selected. This place is fabulous, I know you have loved it, but it is a competition where a single winner represents this great project, you can proudly withdraw that you showed great skills, great knowledge, a great personality, you are a great warrior that in any project that you participate, you will give yourself to the maximum with the great discipline and enthusiasm that belongs to you, the great competitor is withdrawn, it is nostalgic to see the competitors depart, but that is the competences, there is only one representative for this great project, competitors enjoy the great stay in this place, continue to strive for your great project, fight tirelessly, there will be too much time to rest, be happy enjoy the great moments, enjoy what they do, because it is the best gift they can receive, the satisfaction of belonging to great projects that give meaning to their great lives, rest and when they have to fight do it with great force, p so that they realize their great participation, their warrior personality.

We retire many go happy not to be selected, knowing that they have another opportunity to continue fighting. I arrive at my house I go straight to the monitors waiting for the arrival of Florencet, with the great guru, I see her on the monitor, I give her the necessary approach, great guru I retire from this great place and I do not want to leave, it hurts me to leave this place where I was the 3 most wonderful months of my life, if your daughter heard you talk to me with my heart, I am here to help you, it is a great pain that I feel, I do not assimilate my defeat, I had never been in such a beautiful place, that has given me so many things, I feel confused I do not know what to do, I do not know what awaits me outside, daughter in this life there are wonderful experiences that are stuck in our mind, to lose them the duel is not easy, you had a great experience in this place, it is important that you always remember it, that it serves as a background to achieve wonderful things, fear it invades you daughter, many times for situations that did not occur or that we simply imagine that they will happen.

It is important to enjoy life, to know that in our path there are ups and downs, failures, pain, happiness, each emotion has its own lapse of time, it is necessary to enjoy what makes us happy, when the pain comes, it is important to make reality make us live those emotions that affect us, we must not hide, we must face them with true feelings, if you want to cry, do it, if your suffering produces pain, manifest it, do not hide it, in life there are times of happiness and sadness, live those lapses to the fullest, daughter understand your feelings, relax, express all that pain, that affects you, that will make you stronger, never hide your true feelings express them, we are human, we are not immune to pain, scars, disappear, When you let your emotions flow, when you realize what happens, when you express all that pain, when they tell you to be strong, you must be strong, when you fight for your goals. you, not to hide your feelings, that is to be cowardly and it is about your life handling it with courage, expressing your emotions, your feelings, that will give you more value, to achieve your dreams, your desired goals, great guru, I understand you, but what awaits me is outside, daughter awaits you a world full of options, opportunities for development, the great opportunity you had to be in this great place, has given you a great experience, the preparation you took during those 3 months, is to defend yourself against any storm that comes your way, your skills, your strengths have increased, your time in this place has been to obtain the necessary knowledge, to defend yourself against any problem that comes your way.

What you have just experienced is something unique, you are a great leader, you received endless learning, your family and loved ones await you with enthusiasm, throw yourself into life with more strength, you have not lost anything, you have the balance of what you have obtained in this place and you will realize that you have won, analyze everything, turn to the past, just observe yourself as you were before being here, as your personality has changed today, you know that the most important thing in your life is the present, today it is important for you, you know that you will transcend, because today you will face the world with more force, forget fear, you are a warrior that has shown great value, you will be the example of countless people, the world needs leaders like you, I see in you a promising future, I know that whatever comes your way, you will never give up, because you received an advanced philosophy that became wisdom, is the most precious treasure of any leader.

Thank you very much guru, for your great philosophy, you open my mind, a philosophy that I know I received, all I have left is to cultivate that great seed, so that it begins to give the desired fruits that I wish, thank you great guru, for your great words, you give me advice and support to continue my great adventure through life, daughter I send you my blessings, enjoy what life gives you, however insignificant it may seem grateful, all that the universe gives you is with love , receive it, with the maximum discipline and as long as there is gratitude in you, love what you receive with strength, because it is yours, it belongs to you, it is part of your being, thank you great guru, daughter your way is full of surprises and blessings, that will make your life, what you want, never stop dreaming, because miracles exist and arrive when you least expect it.

Florencet retires, I see her face has changed in the time I speak with the great guru, I see her with a semblance of security, great strength, I am amazed, as the guru has the great ability to motivate people, his philosophy spiritual, it's great, because it changes feelings, emotions, contributes to positive motivations, it's very important that they talk to him, the competitors who leave, since their work does not end, a world awaits them, with difficulties, but with great miracles, great challenges, great opportunities, great experiences, today ends this great day, saying goodbye to another great competitor, I will analyze the subjects and the schedule of the next month, this way it would be;

Monday	**Teacher**	**Subject**
8:00 to 10:45	Salomomr	Elite Training I
11:00 to 12:45	Laeva	Global Communication I
12:50 to 13:50	FOOD	
14:00 to 15:45	Teslac	Global Strategic Planning I
16:00 to 17:45	Mcyuretzili	Empathy I
18:00 to 18:55	Edisonic	Vision I
19:00 to 20:00	Noetherli	Transcendental Yoga I

Tuesday	**Teacher**	**Subject**
8:00 to 10:45	Salomomr	Philosophy of Champion and Training I

11:00 to 12:45   Markl Emotional intelligence of
competence I

12:50 to 13:50   FOOD

14:00 to 15:45   Vincir   Focus I

16:00 to 17:45   Curielm   Fortresses I

18:00 to 18:55   Yessica   Self-Realization I

19:00 to 20:00   Noetherli   Transcendental Yoga I

Wednesday	Teacher	Subject
8:00 to 10:45	Yessica	Motivational Training I
11:00 to 12:45	Laeva	Global Communication I
12:50 to 13:50	FOOD	
14:00 to 15:45	Teslac	Global Strategic Planning I
16:00 to 17:45	Mcyuretzili	Empathy I
18:00 to 18:55	Edisonic	Vision I
19:00 to 20:00	Noetherli	Transcendental Yoga I

Thursday	Teacher	Subject

8:00 to 10:45	Salomomr Philosophy of Champion and Training I
11:00 to 12:45	Markl Emotional intelligence of competence I
12:50 to 13:50	FOOD
14:00 to 15:45	Vincir	Focus I
16:00 to 5:45	Curielm	Fortresses I
18:00 to 18:55	Yessica	Self-Realization I
19:00 to 20:00	Noetherli	Transcendental Yoga I

Friday	**Teacher**	**Subject**
8:00 to 10:45	Salomomr	Elite Training I
11:00 to 12:45	Markl	Emotional intelligence of competence I
12:50 to 13:50	FOOD	
14:00 to 15:45	Vincir	Focus I
16:00 to 17:45	Curielm	Fortresses I
18:00 to 18:55	Yessica	Self-Realization I
19:00 to 20:00	Noetherli	Transcendental Yoga I

Saturday	**Teacher**	**Subject**
8:00 a.m. to 5:45 p.m.	Salomomr Yessica	Exploration I
6:00 pm to 8:00 pm	Noetherli	Transcendental Yoga I

Sunday

Strategic rest; with work options according to the needs of the participant.

Important note:

All the subjects are focused, with the project of each competitor.

We start another great month of knowledge, of learning, of new adventures, our visualization increases, the competitors, every month that passes are stronger, more focused, in their strengths and capacities, every day they give themselves to the maximum with the greatest effort.

It was an amazing month, it left us with lots of learning, the subjects, they complement the sophisticated knowledge, which the competitors need to develop their big projects, it is effective to mention, that there is not an easy subject, all have their degrees of difficulty the teachers, they use his maximum effort to transmit the knowledge necessary for the development of the competitors has been a great month, tomorrow is the 4th month, another great competitor will come out, all are nervous, as always nobody wants to retire from this great place, who will be whoever who will retire, I do not know, even the great job of the teachers to select, the next competitor to retire.

I have observed all of them, they are great warriors who do not give up, they fight every day, they know it's a new day, they only think in the present, I go to sleep tomorrow we have a great day, it's Saturday it's 14: 50, I'm about to enter the great hall, all the competitors are present, the professors are on the podium, general observers of all the competitors, who will be the teacher who will mention the retiring competitor, I am Professor Laeva, I am representing all my fellow teachers, to describe this great moment, as we mentioned each ceremony, for us it is a very difficult job, to evaluate them for 3 days, to know the great competitor that retires, we would like everyone to continue this great adventure, but we know the great responsibility of this great project, only one person will be the one that will represent us worldwide, human development is great, requires a lot of responsibility, disciplin a, leadership, courage, dedication, planning.

I mention only a few links but we all know that it is still something else, we dream of a better future, we are aware that to achieve our goals and objectives, sacrifices have to be made, which in advance, we know will be worth forever, due to the great project that will transcend history, we know of the great dedication of each of you, today is a great day, but we know the great responsibility of doing things well, the person who retires, is a great leader, who we know that the learning that you obtained during these 4 months that passed, will be a base for your development, each one of you will have a great profile, which will be a human development obtained, for your development, in the global era that awaits you anxiously , the world needs leaders committed to the great development, the person who retires is a great being who has shown us how to persevere until the last minute, the great competitor who retires from this great place is who earned the respect of all competitors and the recognition of their teachers, the great competitor who withdraws from the competition is;

8.- Name: Joao

Age: 39 years

Brazil country

Profession: Aerospace Engineer

Project: creation of construction materials

Sport: Football

Language: Portuguese, English

Altruism for the world: Collection of garbage and waste, to create resistant materials so that everyone has houses.

The lights are turned on, there is great relief among the competitors, everyone is saying goodbye with a big hug with Joao, even tears are observed, he is a great competitor, in each class he showed that he was a great warrior. Competitors are difficult these moments, but feel the sacrifices as a benefit of a great cause, each one of you, shows your great desires to learn and to be here, but we know that every month someone has to leave, so that it continues in great development. magnificent project, all are great competitors, today that Joao retires, I want to congratulate him, for his great dedication and his constant struggle, a great element is removed, but we continue to build a great project, all the teachers wish you a great way to the success.

Joao retires, changes the face of the competitors, they are seen with great relief, they are reborn, they know they are still in the competition, I imagine by everything I have seen, that every day that passes will increase the profiles, there will be a Special wealth that has been observed since the beginning, the great level of the competitors.

I retire to my house to observe on the monitors this great moment, I observe Joao says; great guru I'm with a lot of nostalgia, it's a hard blow I'm getting, it's going to cost me a lot of work to adapt outside, I've already got used to this great place, it's a great loss in my life, son I know what you're going through, I perceive your feelings, I know that it hurts too much to leave this great place, all the life hurts the losses, more when you adapt to something wonderful, that you had never lived, but son this is the life, recognizes everything you have obtained in this stay, you have a balance of all the good that you take, son today you have another mentality, your positive thoughts have increased, your visualization towards life is different, you know that to reach your goals you have to make many efforts, until you get your dreams, you how you feel but your life is not over.

Accumulate all the extraordinary things that happen in your way, those riches that you obtain will give you strength and support, to continue in the times of crisis, feel happiness because you were 4 months in a place that provided you wisdom and tools, continue your way the light has come to you, the universe is witness that your spirituality has grown, thank you great guru for your wonderful words, I feel that I am reborn more strongly, you are a great light for my way, your wisdom is the water in the desert , gives me encouragement to continue my journey, if in our life there are countless experiences of you depends on what you take, life gives you many options, all you have to do is take advantage of them, always visualize your way with the great mission that you have in your life, always be in the great path of the winners, it is very hard, but with strength, dedication, courage, you can be included in that group.

Develop your skills every day, always prepare for battles, until you win the great war, you know you are a warrior capable of achieving your goals, always dream, visualize, miracles exist, when you least expect it comes the great pleasure of the great miracle achieved, thank you great guru, I feel happier to have listened to you, I know that my job is to strive every day, to achieve my goals, if son, I see in you a great future, observe your great capabilities that characterize you, you have a big road in front of you every day fight with more force, you are a great leader you have shown, use your leadership, for the development of humanity, use your creativity, to develop business, for the benefit of humanity, son your way this full of light, knowledge and wisdom, thank you great guru, a strong hug is given, what great words the guru expresses, his wisdom and spirituality is magnificent, the knowledge he transmits, are for the whole life, even every one that I observe his intervention I learn more about life, on Monday the great classes begin again these are going to be the schedules;

Monday	Teacher	Subject
8:00 to 10:45	Salomomr	Training Elite II
11:00 to 12:45	Laeva	Global Communication II

12:50 to 13:50	FOOD	
14:00 to 15:45 II	Teslac	Global Strategic Planning
16:00 to 17:45	Mcyuretzili	Empathy II
18:00 to 18:55	Edisonic	Vision II
19:00 to 20:00 II	Noetherli	Transcendental Yoga

Tuesday	**Teacher**	**Subject**
8:00 to 10:45	Salomomr	Philosophy of Champion and Training II
11:00 to 12:45	Markl	Emotional intelligence of competence II
12:50 to 13:50	FOOD	
14:00 to 15:45	Vincir	Focus II
16:00 to 17:45	Curielm	Fortresses II
18:00 to 18:55	Yessica	Self-Realization II
19:00 to 20:00	Noetherli	Transcendental Yoga II

Wednesday	**Teacher**	**Subject**
8:00 to 10:45	Yessica	Motivational Training II

11:00 to 12:45	Laeva	Global Communication II
12:50 to 13:50	FOOD	
14:00 to 15:45	Teslac	Global Strategic Planning II
16:00 to 17:45	Mcyuretzili	Empathy II
18:00 to 18:55	Edisonic	Vision II
19:00 to 20:00	Noetherli	Transcendental Yoga II

Thursday	**Teacher**	**Subject**
8:00 to 10:45	Salomomr	Philosophy of Champion and Training II
11:00 to 12:45	Markl	Emotional intelligence of competence II
12:50 to 13:50	FOOD	
14:00 to 15:45	Vincir	Focus II
16:00 to 17:45	Curielm	Fortresses II
18:00 to 18:55	Yessica	Self-Realization II
19:00 to 20:00	Noetherli	Transcendental Yoga II

Friday	**Teacher**	**Subject**
8:00 to 10:45	Salomomr	Training Elite II

11:00 to 12:45   Markl Emotional intelligence of
competence II

12:50 to 13:50   FOOD

14:00 to 15:45   Vincir   Focus II

16:00 to 17:45   Curielm   Fortresses
II

18:00 to 18:55   Yessica   Self-Realization
II

19:00 to 20:00   Noetherli   Transcendental Yoga
II

Saturday   **Teacher**   **Subject**

8:00 a.m. to 5:45 p.m.   Salomomr   Exploration II

                         Yessica

6:00 PM to 8:00 PM   Noetherli   Transcendental Yoga
II

Sunday

Strategic rest; with work options according to the needs of the
participant.

Important note:

All the subjects are focused, with the project of each
competitor.

They continued as always the classes with great knowledge, great experiences and great wisdom, all the competitors have improved a lot, it is difficult to know the next one that is going to retire, everyone is fighting in a way worthy of recognition, I have realized that everything world likes this great place and they are going to sell expensive their defeat, the motivation has increased all are great leaders, all the projects in each class are complemented with more ideas, I imagine, that the next competitor that comes out can be experimenting, with the ideas obtained, how your project can work in the real world, the desire for learning of each competitor is sophisticated, it is a very fruitful exchange of ideas, the third Saturday of the month arrives, another great test, we are in front of the professors .

Professor Yessica speaks, congratulations are great competitors, we know that every day they try their best, all teachers agree in our positive thoughts towards you, they have shown us that they are here for something, today we will do mountaineering, the teacher opens a chest, gives each of the competitors a pair of binoculars, this tool is now part of you, I want you to look to the south to see the exemplary mountain that is observed, in the center there is a banner that flies gigantic white color, with a golden shield, if you observe it, everyone answered yes, there competitors, this is our goal, today it will be team work, the teacher will lead the group, I will go behind all of you, we will be a single group, sometimes we will walk at a rapid pace and in others at a steady pace, we are one, we struggle to reach our goal, each one taking one of their backpacks has their respective names, the content will go using according to the degrees of difficulty.

Competitors have 10 minutes to put their equipment, we will all go out in one step, they will be located according to the step of the teacher, I find my backpack and I put it on, this is great, mountaineering, are majestic sports, observe with binoculars the big mountain is a great goal, competitors ready, it's time to start, the teacher will start, in their brands ready competitors, we started the great adventure, we all go out with great enthusiasm to fill us with the great adventure that awaits us , in our way you see a great flora is a fabulous therapy, I enjoy, I fill my lungs with such a pure air, that enters my interior with an energy that awakens all my senses, I feel the earth under my feet, still wet , there is an impressive network that covers us all the great fauna that we are observing, there are animals that I had never seen, I imagine that they are in danger of extinction, we hear a great sound of birds that sing, my ears are surprised sensory, pleasant sounds that relax me, we continue our way amazed by the great perfume that leaves the nature, I believe that if we lived in this place, it would be our eternal youth, everyone is enjoying this great natural wonder, the animals Savages watch us, as if we were part of them, they do not see intentions of attacking us, as they wish they could not do it because of the great safety net around us.

We have 1:30 minutes of travel, a spectacular thunder is heard, Professor Yessica tells us that we are about to arrive at a big waterfall where we will drink water and have lunch, when we arrive we will see a crowd of people fishing and some chefs, preparing great dishes , we all meet, the teacher tells us that in our team there is a silver cylindrical container, that we take it out and drink the water that falls from the big waterfalls, I am amazed by the landscape that is around us, the waterfalls are full of fish , that they swim in the opposite direction, that is to say that countercurrent, those fish show that their strength is great, since we drank all fresh water, we went to a large table for 30 people, adorned it, all the great dishes that the Chefs, the teacher Yessica tells us that today she will eat all the great products that are on the way, right now all the dishes served are fresh fish , with vegetables and fruit juices from around here, today the chefs, we will be fed with native dishes, with products of our way and what this great place produces, enjoy it, this is something unique.

This place guys is self-sufficient, everything they eat is totally fresh, organic, everything they have eaten are products of this place, enjoy it and good profit, this amazes me is a self-sufficient place, I've known countless places that import their food , this is a great culture that is capable of producing what it consumes and still exports a large part of its products, the chefs, they cooked great, this was a great delicacy, it had never eaten so natural or so natural, nature gives us gifts wonderful, this day I feel nostalgic I had never eaten so relaxed around nature, I hear the sound of the waterfalls the fish, this is something dreamed, something spiritual, after a good time of enjoyment we continue our way, it is amazing the energy that It has given me that great banquet, I feel great, we continue walking amazed by the variety of flowers that adorn our path, this is a dream place, every day that I spend in this I become amazed, every day is wonderful, surprising.

We continue, we have been walking for 3 hours, they all look relaxed, as if it were not an effort to climb the mountain, the teacher tells us to take out our binoculars that we are about to arrive, we can see the flag, but it is the representation of the image I feel we still have about two hours left, we arrive at a surprising place, it is like a barrier that does not allow anyone to pass, the teacher tells us, competitors it's time to use the equipment, in their backpacks there is harness, ropes, go to climb that barrier, I'm going to do the first climb, to reach the top I put the supports to start climbing, it's difficult, but the teacher does it with amazing ability, after 30 minutes, the ropes are already hanging by the great barrier, the teacher has fulfilled the great work, now we have to climb.

The teacher tells us that she will follow us, so that everything is done with the greatest security, I have never climbed up an incline, but there is always a first time, we follow the indications and we begin, we all take a slow step, rest and go back to continue , until little by little we are fulfilling the objective, to dominate the great barrier, when we arrived the teacher was doing sit-ups, he tells us that in what we went up he was doing an exercise routine, which provides strength, all of us arrived exhausted almost with the heart in the hands, in reality, climbing are short distances, but where much force is used, we achieve the goal, we all hydrate, the teacher gives us 5 minutes to return to our path, we continue walking, we are close to the goal .

The teacher tells us to follow this step to arrive in 40 minutes, the air pressure increases, breathing becomes difficult, but it is great, as climbing the barrier gave us more strength, we continue our way, with great energy, after for a while, we already see the splendid flag, it is a great satisfaction, to fulfill the objective, we all touch the flagpole, knowing that we have arrived, it is shocking what we see ahead, it is the top of the mountain, but it does not end there there are still more mountains, but we have a great view of 360 degrees, there is a building, that shines its brightness, around the chefs, they wait for us with a feast of delicious food, there is an orchestra that plays a special music, it is so motivating music, which gives us great joy to find ourselves in that place, a chef addresses us and indicates us; the dishes that are going to taste, is meat of exotic animals, there are people who are dedicated to raising them, with a healthy, organic diet, they have the best growing conditions, enjoy the great dishes that we have just served at the table, we wish that be of your great pleasure, enjoy them, we have done them, with great enthusiasm and joy, the great test they did today, have their reward, begin to enjoy, we all sit at the big table, are great dishes, such soft flesh that melt in your mouth, its flavor is great, they are unique delicacies that we had never tasted, today we have the privilege to try, a minimum part, of nature.

As we finish, the teacher tells us that in 20 minutes he wants to see the 6th floor of the building, since we are there, the two professors are at the center of the room, Professor Yessica speaks, competitors today as always was a great day, our great challenge, has been fulfilled, everyone enjoyed the challenge, I know that nature enriched its path and the extraordinary dishes prepared by the chefs, were energetic for their bodies, another objective has been achieved, I am proud to belong to this great group , of unbreakable warriors, then the teacher will talk to you about;

The great top

Our beginnings were uncertain, but with only one objective, to reach the top.

It was fabulous our way, of enjoyment and enjoyment.

Many passages passed through our minds, where we could give up.

But we continued, our spirit wanted to achieve something wonderful.

The path gave us the sensory facility to activate all our senses.

The prizes that we were getting in our way, taught us that we should always be sensitive.

Sweat ran through our body, the sun was our faithful companion, the shadow sheltered us.

The smells that we perceived, brought us closer to our goal.

When we climbed, we thought we would fall, but the force that surrounded us made us see ahead.

All the objectives of our life, take a step, a beginning, a path.

Working as a team gave us a special strength, we were one, our lights became a sun.

We realize that, with work, discipline and dedication, everything can be achieved.

The ability to achieve our goals gives us a profile of facing any challenge.

When we were close to the goal, we looked forward to finishing the big moment with all our might.

When we touched the flagpole, it was like touching a part of the sky.

When we reached the goal, we turned around and realized that the road was still extensive.

We realized that the objectives do not end there, that there are still more challenges.

The great summit, taught us, that when we have achieved the desired, another challenge is already present.

It means that our constant struggle never ends, that the day our bodies rest, it will be when we cease to exist.

The fabulous thing is that we are aware that yesterday's success is there, that our mentality must always be aware that work continues.

The great summit was our happiness, it made us smile, it gave us freedom.

Our dreams come true, with a great miracle that we can not believe.

We have to be always active, so that our bodies are always jovial, full of energy.

The great summit, gave us breath, gave us the great prize of recognizing, its great difficulty.

We find a great profile, upon reaching our goal, that enthusiasm is tireless.

That when you reach your goal, you find that it is time to enjoy the most, the great moment.

The great summit, gives us the spiritual philosophy, that the challenges never end.

The great summit teaches us that there are still more mountains to explore, more roads to travel.

The great summit taught me an infinity of skills, but the main one was that it made me more spiritual.

The great summit was a great battle, but we know that to win the war we have to continue persevering day by day.

The great summit, gave us knowledge, gave us a part of wisdom.

The great summit was our goal.

The great summit, was our love.

Competitors enjoy this great moment, what they have just done is an experience for their life, in 1 hour we retire from this great place, we will meet in the central courtyard, some all-terrain vehicles, will take us to the stadium, having a great stay, what great words of the teachers and if it is reality, every day we have unique experiences that accumulate for our growth, we go to the massage area we want to consent to recover our energies, I finish this wonderful day, it was a unique experience.

Today, Saturday marks 5 months, when the competition began, in a few minutes, we will know who is the next competitor to retire, all these months have been great, of a lot of learning, of extraordinary experiences, we have been in a great place that we never imagined, this place has left its mark in our hearts, in our spirits, the universe is witness of the impressions that this place has caused to our lives, I am directed to the room where the teachers, have the great task of deciding who is the one who retires, they are in front of us, Professor Vincir takes the floor; big competitors we are gathered, to tell you which one of you is the next one who is retiring from this great competition, I have the honor of speaking on behalf of my colleagues, it has been a very hard work that we have had to carry out, it has been 3 days in those who all their teachers have put all their experience, to make the difficult selection, during life, we have many tests, since our beginnings in school we have always been evaluated, it is something that never ends, because in the end, the maximum evaluation they are going to have is the life, everyone in their exams have gone great, have amazed all our expectations, theoretically and practically we know of their delivery, we observe a special feeling, of realization, they are great competitors, who are willing to deliver your life to this great place, I recognize your work, your discipline, your delivery, the level of competition is very high, started from the lowest, until the day e today in the place they are, for us nostalgia is created in our minds, but we all know that great sacrifices give us great rewards, that is what we are looking for, that is our great objective, to obtain the most precious treasure of wisdom , to share it with the world population, our work is unique in history, for that reason it must be done with excellence and quality.

I love the level of competition, this level is what supports the exchange of ideas, feedback, the creation of a set of brilliant minds, with the same goal, spirituality has made us transcend, the universe is witness, our creative and innovative work, for that reason I am the spokesman of my colleagues, the person who retires is, a great human being who was a pride of all, but we know that the capacity is often not measured accurately, for such a situation it is important, keep growing day by day, we are human beings that constantly, we are developing, in this place they manifested what they came with facts, but this is life, the great road we are building has to continue, the next competitor that retires is an individual that his spiritual state illuminated our hearts, his presence motivated us to continue, he taught us that he is a great warrior willing to sacrifice to achieve his goals, the Great competitor that retires is;

4.- Name: Giselle

Age: 31 years

Country: Germany

Profession: Psychologist

Project: Create a positive mindset around the world

Sport: Athletics

Language: English, German, French.

Altruism for the world: Indicate and follow up on personal strengths

You hear all your data, we all cry, but that is the level of competence, also the great warriors have to go, the teacher continues, competitors I will read this great epitaph called;

Power transforms

The great responsibility, hit our backs, making our way slower.

Time was witness, that load was made lighter, until it disappeared.

The road taught me, countless options, I experimented until I found the right ones.

My path lit up, the darkness disappeared, but sometimes it came back stronger.

My work began to bear fruit, experience, wisdom.

My energy came out strongly, it taught me to be more persevering.

When the power came to me, it was an impressive force, which allowed me to put obstacles aside.

Power transforms, it is like the great rock, which with work and love became sculpture.

At night came the big dreams, which made me continue.

The failures were painful, but in the end they taught me how I should not do things.

Love came to me, taught me that when you love what you do, time disappears.

Power transforms, it is the creativity that came, after so much sacrifice.

Visualization taught me to think about my goal day by day, until I saw that dream come true.

When tiredness appeared, my mind bravely asked me to continue with greater strength.

My work team, they saw me as a great warrior, they began to imitate me, we grew up together.

Power transforms, the great skills that, obtained, are summarized in wisdom.

The motivation taught me, that when the ruins are there, we must move the rubble to continue.

My tears taught me that they were healthy, because it was important to express the pain I felt.

My achievement was infinite, when I began to see the results, however simple they were, they filled my soul and my heart.

Power transforms, being grateful taught me, it is a way of living brilliantly and wonderfully unique.

My dreams came true, I became more spiritual and I knew that miracles exist.

My life is a great miracle, every detail is surprising, even then I think it is not real, it is a dream.

I realized that the impossible can be made possible, believing in the great miracles of life.

Power transforms life.

Power transforms humanity.

Power transforms the universe.

Competitors go on their way as great gladiators, waiting for the next battle, continue with strength, energy and love, are bases of human development, lead by example, be leaders, but great leaders, you hear great applause, Giselle retires , there is a pain of nostalgia, but at the same time a great tranquility of not being selected, I go to my house to observe the monitors, I arrive is Giselle, with the great guru, daughter tell me your feelings I am to listen to you, release the crying , great guru this is a nightmare, I can not control my negative emotions, my legs tremble, I feel defeated, daughter is normal what you feel, I know you had gotten used to the great routine of this great place.

The loss you feel at this moment is unbearable, daughter nobody wants to leave here, we know that all humans love things that give us meaning, that enrich our lives, your profile is great you have developed skills that you never imagined, feel the pride that you are another woman, a woman more focused on what you want, your future is great, only, you have to be like you were in this place a great warrior, your family will see you with great pride, you have to keep striving for Do what you love, that is your only job, find the job you fall in love with, be ready to give your life to what you love without receiving any money, you will realize that when you find the goal you want, your happiness will be so great you will forget about the economic and this will appear as magic, your wealth will be infinite, love what you do with great strength, that is the great key, for the achievement of great goals.

Great guru I love to talk with you, you are such a spiritual person, that you give a great sense to my life, my soul wakes up, I feel your words in my heart, great guru thank you for waking me up again, I am going to face the world with great strength, I carry in my mind your great advice, daughter breathe deep, you are free, do what you want, with strength, energy, discipline, creativity, fight for what you want, when you find your goal, your goals will be visible forever, be spiritual, you are observed by the great universe, feel proud for your great way in this beautiful land, take advantage of all the opportunities that come your way, it will be great every time you achieve what you want, it was a pleasure to meet you, they embrace, Giselle retires.

It is a great feeling that transports to the great human understanding, to the great mentality that moves spirits and hearts, it is important every detail of feeling expressed by each competitor, all feel the maximum pain of leaving this great place and I understand them, for what I have talked with all the competitors, none have lived an experience like this, all have explained to me their great astonishment of being in this great place, they all say that it is a great dream they do not want to wake up, the scenario where this competition is taking place is great, the teachers are great with their knowledge, the great wisdom that they transmit to us is getting stuck in our minds, our minds have developed in a great way, the sport has complemented us, in a wonderful way, that we all feel different people that when we arrived, our development has increased, it is great, all the experiences that we have lived day by day, the great foods that and they give us, as they treat us, all this makes the competitors try their best, all the philosophy they transmit us cultivates our spirit, good to rest from this great day.

CHAPTER VI

Classes begin tomorrow, the organization is as follows;

Monday	Teacher	Subject
8:00 to 10:45	Salomomr	Training Elite III
11:00 to 12:45	Laeva	Global Communication III
12:50 to 13:50	FOOD	
14:00 to 15:45	Teslac	Global Strategic Planning III
16:00 to 17:45	Mcyuretzili	Empathy III
18:00 to 18:55	Edisonic	Vision III
19:00 to 20:00	Noetherli	Transcendental Yoga III

Tuesday	Teacher	Subject
8:00 to 10:45 Training III	Salomomr	Philosophy of Champion and
11:00 to 12:45 competence III	Markl	Emotional intelligence of
12:50 to 13:50 FOOD		
14:00 to 15:45	Vincir	Focus III
16:00 to 17:45 III	Curielm	Fortresses
18:00 to 18:55 III	Yessica	Self-Realization
19:00 to 20:00 III	Noetherli	Transcendental Yoga

Wednesday	Teacher	Subject
8:00 to 10:45 III	Yessica	Motivational Training
11:00 to 12:45 III	Laeva	Global Communication
12:50 to 13:50 FOOD		
14:00 to 15:45 III	Teslac	Global Strategic Planning
16:00 to 17:45	Mcyuretzili	Empathy III
18:00 to 18:55	Edisonic	Vision III

19:00 to 20:00 III   Noetherli   Transcendental Yoga

Thursday	Teacher	Subject
8:00 to 10:45 Training III	Salomomr Philosophy of Champion and	
11:00 to 12:45 competence III	Markl Emotional intelligence of	
12:50 to 13:50	FOOD	
14:00 to 15:45	Vincir	Focus III
16:00 to 17:45	Curielm	Fortresses III
18:00 to 18:55	Yessica	Self-Realization III
19:00 to 20:00 III	Noetherli	Transcendental Yoga

Friday	Teacher	Subject
8:00 to 10:45 Training	Salomomr	Elite III
11:00 to 12:45 competence III	Markl Emotional intelligence of	
12:50 to 13:50	FOOD	
14:00 to 15:45	Vincir	Focus III

16:00 to 17:45	Curielm	Fortresses III
18:00 to 18:55	Yessica	Self-Realization III
19:00 to 20:00	Noetherli	Transcendental Yoga III

Saturday	**Teacher**	**Subject**
8:00 a.m. to 5:45 p.m.	Salomomr	Exploration III
	Yessica	
6:00 p.m. to 8:00 p.m.	Noetherli	Transcendental Yoga III

Sunday

Strategic rest; with work options according to the needs of the participant.

Important note:

All the subjects are focused, with the project of each competitor.

The classes continued, the teachers with their great efforts, the competitors developed their skills, their leadership grew, the love for their project transcended. He spent this month very quickly with his great degrees of difficulty, with his wonderful classes, it is fantastic to be in this great place, our knowledge grows, it is spectacular to be in a place where every day you learn something new.

Today is Saturday the last of the month within 10 minutes, I'm about to enter the great hall, where the teachers will indicate who is the next to leave, I enter the great room, the great ceremony begins, Professor Salomomr rises, great competitors is For me it is an honor to be in this great place that inspires a special light, that illuminates any heart, we did a great job together with the professors to designate who is the next participant who retires from this great competition, I want to tell you at this moment that I admire them all, they are great warriors. It is a privilege and honor to work with you, I see the light of each one of you, how great they react in the trainings and we agree with the teachers that they are wonderful and special students, it is gratifying to work with you, but I have to mention to the next one that he retires is a great warrior who has shown by example, he because he is in this great place, it was great work With all the team and especially with this great warrior, it is a great satisfaction, knowing the dedication of each one of you, it is a great legacy, it is a great example, the next warrior who retires, is someone who surrendered all his efforts in a single package, his sweat was lost in the earth manifesting his great capabilities, his great hunger for triumph, the great competitor who retires from this grandiose scenario is;

9.- Name: Winstond

   Age: 30 years

   Country: England

   Profession: Chef

Project: Quality food

Sport: Rugby

Language: English, Spanish, French

Altruism for the world: Create worldwide feeding centers for the population in general.

My great admiration for you Winstond, I know you should not go out, but in this great place you have to make great sacrifices, thank you for your great determination, for your courage, continue your path with great success, we all embrace it, retire sad and with his eyes on the ground, he can not believe it, after his great speech by the professor, the grand ceremony ends, I retire a little hurriedly, I urgently observe in the monitors, the feelings and the reaction of Winstond, I arrive at the monitor, is coming towards the great guru, son ahead you are in your great house of blessings, tell me I hear you, great guru I feel die, is released in tears vanishes until you are stuck, Why? If everything went so well.

Son there are occasions in the spiritual sense that we have to die, to live, what does this mean, that if we fought in our battles of life, as if we were going to die, they would be great, we would fight with great force, we would be impressive, we would know that it is a supernatural power that moves us, that the universe gives us a special courage where fatigue never comes, we can rest until we achieve our great goal, you must live the present to the fullest and get the great message of the past or the extraordinary things that you have lived, you have to transport them to the present, with the ability and joy to get them, it is gratifying to be a champion, if you do not succeed, it is fantastic to have given the maximum effort with the great possibility of achieving the desired goal, Son the future smiled at you, but you should know that it is uncertain, but I recommend what you learned, that is your path, you have achieved a new place full of light, it is the It's about your thoughts, dreams and achievements.

Show out there that you are another, that you are a great warrior that emerged from nothing, you have sophisticated tools that make you a great leader, you know that each day is different, that each day will be new for you, you will face with enthusiasm, courage, understanding that you are going to transcend, because you have belonged to a great project and have contributed for 6 long months, where you learned, it was great, you got a special wisdom, that you can apply anywhere, the guru touches your forehead, sees an immense light, is receiving a great energy, gets up, thank you very much guru, that I feel good, with a special and pure energy, that is in my whole body, thank you great guru, for your great words, I feel better, all my emotions that affected me came out, son I give you my blessings, continue your path, with greater strength, you have great abilities, your intellect increased, your maturity is excellent, walks with energy and decision, that pal open those of the great guru, another competitor, who left a great legacy of knowledge and ways of acting with determination, to rest that great day, I will dream of all the great moments, I know I will not finish, because they are too many .

Tomorrow is Monday, the seventh month begins, as we are going forward, these are the subjects and schedules that will be taught;

Monday	Teacher	Subject
8:00 to 10:45		Salomomr Training Elite Special Forces I

11:00 to 12:45   Laeva Intrapersonal and interpersonal communication I

12:50 to 13:50   FOOD

14:00 to 15:45   Teslac   Global Strategic Mission I

16:00   to 17:45   McYuretzili   Self-esteem and perception I

18:00 to 18:55   Edisonic Opportunities of transcendence I

19:00 to 20:00   Noetherli   Yoga universal I

Tuesday	**Teacher**	**Subject**
8:00 to 10:45	Salomomr	Skill Growth and Training I
11:00 a 12:45	Markl	Globalized social intelligence I
12:50 to 13:50	FOOD	
14:00 to 15:45	Vincir	Human strategic development I
16:00 to 17:45	Curielm	Integral image development I
18:00 to 18:55	Yessica	Extrinsic and intrinsic motivation I
19:00 to 20:00	Noetherli	Yoga Universal I

Wednesday	Teacher	Subject
8:00 to 10:45	Yessica	Extrinsic and Intrinsic Motivation I
11:00 to 12:45	Laeva	Intrapersonal and interpersonal communication I
12:50 to 13:50	FOOD	
14:00 to 15:45	Teslac	Global Strategic Mission I
16:00 to 17:45	McYuretzili	Self-esteem and perception I
18:00 to 18:55	Edisonic	Opportunities of transcendence I
19:00 to 20:00	Noetherli	Yoga universal I

Thursday	Teacher	Subject
8:00 to 10:45	Salomomr	Skill Growth and Training I
11:00 a 12:45	Markl	Globalized social intelligence I
12:50 to 13:50	FOOD	
14:00 to 15:45	Vincir	Human strategic development I
16:00 to 17:45	Curielm	Integral image development I
18:00 to 18:55	Yessica	Extrinsic and intrinsic motivation I
19:00 to 20:00	Noetherli	Yoga Universal I

Friday	Teacher	Subject
8:00 to 10:45 I	Salomomr	Training Elite Special Forces
11:00 a 12:45 I	Markl	Globalized social intelligence
12:50 to 13:50	FOOD	
14:00 to 15:45 I	Vincir	Human strategic development
16:00 to 17:45 I	Curielm	Integral image development
18:00 to 18:55 I	Yessica	Extrinsic and intrinsic motivation
19:00 to 20:00	Noetherli	Yoga Universal I

Saturday	Teacher	Subject
8:00 a.m. to 5:45 p.m.	Salomomr	Entrepeneur Deportivo de Elite I
	Yessica	
18:00 to 20:00	Noetherli	Yoga Universal I

Sunday

Strategic rest; with work options according to the needs of the participant.

Important note:

All the subjects are focused, with the project of each competitor.

Start training again with more sophisticated materials, it is important to have tools of this type, that show us a great way, to be great explorers of knowledge. They are intense weeks no competitor gives up, they know that fighting day to day to the fullest, their prospects of transcending grow, comes the third Saturday the teachers are at the center to give us their great material Entrepeneur Deportivo Elite I, says Professor Salomomr, competitors it is a happiness to see them again, under this exit of the great sun, its rays illuminate us, penetrate our body, fill it with energy for the next challenge, the universe is witness of our great work day by day, the proof is as follows;

1.- We will swim 2,000 meters in the river, the signaling indicates the distance.

2.- Run half marathon (13,1 miles).

3.- ¿? Will be pending.

Competitors, these will be the great challenges, transition 2 will be 13,1 miles uphill, the goal here will be at the top of the mountain, the transition number 3 will be a big surprise for you, when we reach the top we will be deciphering that great paradigm. Competitors the teacher will give the start, young people in 5 minutes will start the big challenge, competitors ready a shot sounds, we all come out with a huge energy, we all have realized that this is the secret of the elite athletes, go out in competitions with great intensity, so that the heart and vital signs, get used to the great effort and as time goes by, the speed increases, the reaction time and fatigue is bearable.

We are all aware of the great enthusiasm we project, we are all great athletes, ready to give all the necessary efforts. We all completed stage 1. We almost arrived at the same time, we put the next team and run, it's great to hear the heartbeat, I feel great, I feel more alive, it's special and wonderful for me, to be in this great place, the race is intense, but it is a lot of effort, the climb is intense, the effort is great, the air that enters through my lungs is gratifying, we all have the same rhythm, the time goes on we go up, this seems to have no end, after great efforts are reaching the top, the good thing that the teachers, indicated that today is not competition, we have to keep a pace, today what was going to be measured in us is the resistance, we go at kilometer 18, we almost achieved the objective.

We do not know the great surprise that teachers have, with stage 3, it is great to perform this type of exercise, which is done by special forces, it is great to approach the goal, but at the same time unpredictable, which is what awaits us, We all begin to feel the great fatigue, but we wake up the last kilometer that is missing, we all recover energy, we are willing to die, to achieve our goal, the teachers won us by 50 meters, but it was great we met the goal , we arrive at the goal, there is a plane track, there are two beautiful airplanes, they tell us that they use fuel, they use solar energy, the futuristic technology that this place has, they are a great example for the world. that we will do 30 minutes of stretching, with the strategy of removing the lactic acid from our bodies, since we finished the great repair of our body, with the wonderful stretches, the teacher addresses everybody, competitors, we are proud to have fulfilled the great goal that we set for ourselves this day, we are a great group that shows it with facts, I have to point out the test;

3.- Throw ourselves to 5,000 feet of height (1524 meters) in parachute, that gigantic plane that you are observing is the one that will fulfill our dream, achieve that great goal.

All received the necessary training for this great challenge, what we did not tell them was when they were going to need that knowledge, today is the great day that we had to transcend, turn on the plane and tell us to climb, to enter the sophisticated plane, we all we put the equipment that will save our lives, competitors in 5 minutes we will launch, count 15 seconds after the first one is launched and so on until the plane is empty, I throw myself into the great wonderful sky, that my God, I count until 15 and I pull the powerful rope, I feel like dying, my parachute comes out with a power that pulls me up, what an experience, my God, this is dying to live, we see ourselves as great birds in the sky, it is a great parade, we are 8 great birds goodbye in the great sky, it is wonderful, a unique experience, full of adrenaline, I felt that my heart was coming out of fear, but right now I am here in this great place, being the owner of all my Around, I would do it again, tears come out is a great emotion, I never thought to live this great adventure, thank God for this great miracle.

We landed on a large flat plain, covered with grass, which waits for us like a big mattress, what a delight it is to risk to enjoy great moments, we are all in the same place in a great circle, we are all retiring the great equipment, that saved our lives , the fall is spectacular, you must have strength in your legs to cushion the blow, when you step on the ground you must walk, even run, to withstand the great inertia, it is a unique and great experience, since we take off the equipment we are in the form of u before our professors, Professor Yessica speaks, competitors, a great congratulations have fulfilled their great test, this will be a day remembered by all of you, life is made of wonderful things and this is one of them, they have to tell their families and to your future generations of how beautiful life is, the great challenges strengthen us, I am proud to belong to a great team like you, it is gratifying to begin a new day at their side, I see them as my family, their human side contagious, their strength, energy, perseverance, infect me and make me stronger, when we are not together I will miss them, but I will take them the biggest part of my heart, forever, we are going to give ourselves a big applause, with force, that our spirits, our souls, that the universe is witness of our gratitude, that gave us a great day of life and made us dream , with you the great teacher Salomomr, competitors already said the teacher is a great pride to work with you, for that reason I am going to read the following thought called;

Adrenalin

Your word came to my mind, as something natural, something unknown.

I saw you as something normal, like one more phrase.

My heart did not understand your great meaning.

Your value was unknown to me, I knew you existed, but it was normal.

Until I met you, you entered my veins, you explored my body.

Meeting you was the best thing that ever happened to me, in my life.

When I felt your word in my body, I felt alive.

Claro scared me, I could not help it, but when you arrived, that fear became power.

I knew you were a hormone, but I did not know that you produced great power, blood pressure and my heart rate increased.

My muscles were activated, my body was filled with an inexplicable energy.

Depression and sadness buried in my way, thanks Adrenalina.

My confidence returned, my thoughts appeared more strongly, giving me creativity.

You made my body react easily, my strength surprised me.

The energy filled my body, gave me ease, agility, perseverance, helped me to dream.

I realize the greatness of our body, the great natural chemicals it produces.

I am amazed, of the great fantastic machine that belongs to us.

Its value is incalculable, I feel fortunate, the richness of my body belongs to me.

When I practice sports with energy, it produces a fantastic well-being.

Adrenaline that you came to my life, demonstrating your great natural power.

Adrenaline that you taught me that there was a spiritual power.

Adrenaline taught me that there are wonderful things that complement my life.

Adrenaline you gave meaning to my life, you made me know love.

Effective neurotransmitter adrenaline, that you do magic in whatever body you find.

Adrenaline gave me life, teaching me a new world.

Adrenaline, you make changes in my life, the energy came back to me.

Adrenaline, your encounter has given me meaning has filled me with spirituality.

Adrenaline, knowing that before I knew your fear I invaded.

Adrenaline, when I met you, experience the best that has happened in my life.

Adrenaline, great adrenaline are in my heart.

Adrenaline, my energy has awakened all my senses, I feel in communication with the universe.

Adrenaline, thank you for entering my blood, go through my body and transmit to my heart.

Adrenaline, the great sense that you gave to my life, is an incomparable wealth.

Adrenaline, I'm grateful, life is great and wonderful.

 Competitors thank you for being in this great moment, fighting and striving, for being better, we are inspired by this great day, only the universe knows our feelings, what goes through our minds, our spiritual sense, that solar helicopter that they are seeing will transport us , to a great place where we will be spoiled, to recover that energy that we have left, boys to our great transport vehicle, we all climb, our faces can not believe what we have lived, they are amazing situations that enrich our lives, we arrive at the place is a huge building, with a spectacular futuristic structure, I did not just amaze, every day there is something new that surprises me, we go to the great place to bathe and enjoy a great massage, all this is a great prize, as we are treated an incomparable, wonderful way, we introduce ourselves to the place of the chefs, the great cuisine, I'm starving, the dishes are great, what's more I am surprised that all the raw material is generated by this great place, it is sophisticated, with the development that accounts, they do not use pesticides or chemical materials to sow, everything is done as in the past, in a native way, in a great natural way and still They have the privilege of exporting these products to all their organizations in the world.

What a delight, I would work for them only, that they would give me these great dishes to eat, I would feel well served and well paid, we finished the sacred food, every day the chefs, they try to surprise us, their cuisine is delicious, nutritious, fantastic, never in my life had I eaten so brilliantly and constantly, everything in this place is wonderful, when I'm not here, it will be engraved in my mind, like a great experience unique in my life, they tell us to climb again to the great helicopter, the machine transport us to the great stadium, where is our great meeting point, we reach the great stadium, the teacher tells us, competitors, dream of this great moment, because every day is different, great, unique and unrepeatable, rest relax, dream , because miracles exist, we all retire that incredible place, what we do unimaginable, unpredictable, sophisticated things, that give us a great sense of fighting each day with more force.

It is Saturday, the last of the month, in 15 minutes we will know the next competitor who retires, how hard is this moment, but necessary for the great growth of the project, I imagine how are the competitors, nobody wants to retire, nobody wants to leave this great dream and nobody wants to wake up from that great dream. We enter the great hall, the attentive professors observe us; I am Professor Noetherli, representing all the panel of professors who are here by my side, before all deserved recognition to all the competitors, the competition levels have increased, for us it is more complicated every day to select the great competitor that retires, but that is our great job, to make the most sophisticated evaluations, for 3 days so that our work gives us the expected results, the integration of a large group for us was a great responsibility, from the beginning it has become difficult the selection, because they are all great competitors, but we all know our philosophy, make sacrifices, to reach our goals, the next great competitor that retires is, a great human being who showed us a great path of perseverance, teaching us how to do it do things and that we should never give up, on behalf of the great teachers I have to mention the great gladiator who retires today is a magnificent person who gave everything on the battlefield, the great warrior who retires from this wonderful place is;

6.- Name: Queenie

Age: 37 years

Country: Australia

Profession: Telecommunications Engineer

Project: Avoid climate change

Sport: Swimming

Language: English, Greek, Italian

Altruism for the world: through telecommunications, create programs around the world for natural and economic wealth.

This day is transcendent the great sacrifices are for a great cause our Mission, to eliminate the world poverty, give a great applause to your companion, express your feelings, retire a great competitor. We all express our feelings, there are tears, true expressions, great emotions invaded us, we would like no one to leave, but that is the goal to develop the great project, Queenie retires, for that great tunnel full of light, competitors I invite you to follow striving every day more, we are almost at the grand finale of this competition, but there is still a lot of work to be done, surrender to the maximum to their great projects we have to benefit the world population, who needs our help, have a great and wonderful day .

We retired from the big event, many breathe relieved, and have been in this great place for 7 months and I know that no one wants to leave, they are going to sell expensive their defeat, I see in their face that they will fight harder, I retire to my house , I have to observe the monitors, Queenie arrived, is climbing the great mountain to see the great guru, daughter forward you are in your house, this great spiritual temple that belongs to you, thank you great guru, what can I say, tell daughter what you feel , what your soul and your heart express, I am to listen to you and help you, in the great way you have formed, great guru I feel a big lump in my throat the words are gone, if your daughter expresses herself let your emotions emerge with strength, you have to take out everything that bothers you, if great guru, I know, the first thing I thought, when I get to see my relatives, what I tell them is here, I feel defeated.

Daughter the first thing that your family will say when they see you will be happiness, you are their pride, for them you are a great champion, observe the effort you made day by day was exemplary, you motivated your companions to move forward, but daughter this is life, what What if I tell you that fate, if you continue with that great mentality that characterizes you, you will receive countless surprises from life, countless options that will enrich your path, your warrior personality, wage many infantry battles that will make you grow and when face the stormy roads, you will not be afraid, because life and the great experiences you have lived, have given you a magnificent profile of struggle, life smiles at you, the universe is witness to your great efforts day after day, moment after moment, you have lost the notion of time and that is fortifying, daughter miracles exist, in the course of your life you have realized the miracles that have happened to you, they are magnificent and inesper adas, that have come your way when you least expected it, live life to the fullest, as if it were the last day that you were on earth, gives a lot of love, love is the key to open the door of the universe, the great sense towards spirituality, receive the gifts of life, with gratitude, give meaning to the wonderful things in life, learn from failures, be a great woman, proud to do the things you love, dedicate your life to the work of which you are In love, that will give meaning to your life.

Thank you great guru, you are awakening me with a great spiritual sense, you are right I must be grateful, for having stepped on this great place for 7 months, it was a unique, great, incomparable experience, I am going to take the great notes that life has given me, the great chapters that have given me incalculable emotions, the fantastic of life is important to live it to the fullest, I will take as a priority to be always happy and produce happiness, you see daughter you are too intelligent person, you quickly grasp the sense of experiences, daughter enjoys the great moments of your life, I know how you are a great woman, but strive every day to be better, forget time, you only live the day as if it were the last, thank you great guru, embrace, Queenie retires, his body shines with a special light, a great warrior goes away, but a great project is the one that remains, good to rest have been bright days, days of great experiences, unique days.

It is Sunday afternoon, tomorrow the new month begins, these are the subjects that will be taught;

Monday   **Teacher**   **Subject**

8:00 to 10:45   Salomomr Special Forces Training Elite II

11:00 to 12:45 Laeva Intrapersonal and interpersonal communication II

12:50 to 13:50   FOOD

14:00 to 15:45   Teslac   Global Strategic Mission II

16:00 to 17:45   McYuretzili Self-esteem and perception II

18:00 to 18:55		Edisonic Opportunities of transcendence II
19:00 to 20:00	Noetherli	Yoga Universal II

Tuesday	**Teacher**	**Subject**
8:00 to 10:45		Salomomr Skills Growth and Training II
11:00 to 12:45		Markl Globalized Social Intelligence II
12:50 to 13:50 FOOD		
14:00 to 15:45		Vincir Human strategic development II
16:00 to 17:45		Curielm Integral Image Development II
18:00 to 18:55		Yessica extrinsic and intrinsic motivation II
19:00 to 20:00	Noetherli	Yoga Universal II

Wednesday	**Teacher**	**Subject**
8:00 to 10:45		Yessica extrinsic and intrinsic motivation II
11:00 to 12:45		Laeva Intrapersonal and interpersonal communication II

12:50 to 13:50   FOOD

14:00 to 15:45   Teslac   Global Strategic Mission II

16:00 to 17:45   McYuretzili Self-esteem and perception II

18:00 to 18:55   Edisonic Opportunities of transcendence II

19:00 to 20:00   Noetherli   Yoga Universal II

Thursday	Teacher	Subject

8:00 to 10:45   Salomomr   Skills Growth and Training II

11:00 to 12:45   Markl   Globalized Social Intelligence II

12:50 to 13:50   FOOD

14:00 to 15:45   Vincir   Human strategic development II

16:00 to 17:45   Curielm   Integral Image Development II

18:00 to 18:55   Yessica extrinsic and intrinsic motivation II

19:00 to 20:00   Noetherli   Yoga Universal II

Friday	**Teacher**	**Subject**
8:00 to 10:45	Salomomr	Special Forces Training Elite II
11:00 to 12:45	Markl	Globalized Social Intelligence II
12:50 to 13:50	FOOD	
14:00 to 15:45	Vincir	Human strategic development II
16:00 to 17:45	Curielm	Integral Image Development II
18:00 to 18:55	Yessica	extrinsic and intrinsic motivation II
19:00 to 20:00	Noetherli	Yoga Universal II

Saturday	**Teacher**	**Subject**
8:00 a.m. to 5:45 p.m.	Salomomr	Entrepeneur Deportivo de Elite II
	Yessica	
6:00 p.m. to 8:00 p.m.	Noetherli	Yoga Universal II

Sunday

Strategic rest; with work options according to the needs of the participant.

Important note:

All the subjects are focused, with the project of each competitor.

We receive the great and sophisticated classes, all competitors are increasing their capabilities, their strength grows, their energy is spectacular, their motivation, their visualization and all identify with the great mission that awaits the winner.

It is Saturday, the last of the month, in 20 minutes they will tell us who is retiring from the competitors, now I sincerely observe several nervous people and I understand it is not easy to be exposed to be the next one who retires from this great competition, all the teachers in the center of the great podium, and every time the public room looks more empty, there are fewer competitors, the atmosphere becomes a little more tense, we know that nobody wants to retire.

A deep but direct voice is heard in the whole room, I am your servant Professor Teslac, it is a privilege to meet the professors and the great group of competitors that are still fighting, it is a necessity for me to express my admiration, they are a great group that are in the place they deserve, I thank them for their constant struggle, their determination, their focus on achievement, their human sense to collaborate for the benefit of the world population, they have been great students, the feedback has been so great and the illumination of knowledge, of knowing that we are on the right path, also my great respect to all the professors who have fulfilled their great knowledge, this is a great community, where wisdom will be the most precious treasure that will transcend, it touches me the great responsibility of indicating who is the next competitor to retire, the next one is, who fought every day to be better, who gave us a legacy of how to achieve the greatest wishes, but we know that we are in a competition to do something that will make a world history, which will be written in the great pages and chapters of the story, from us depends the effectiveness, the next great student who retires from this wonderful place is, someone we would like him to stay, because we know that his place earned it, for the great achievements, for his great motivations, the great competitor that retires is;

3.- Name: Joharim

Age: 29 years

Country: South Africa

Profession: Master in International Business

Project: Work for everyone

Sport: Cycling

Language: English, German, Portuguese.

Altruism for the world: create jobs to benefit all societies.

We know of the great responsibility that we have under our shoulders, our motto is to make sacrifices for the benefit of the great project, say goodbye to your great companion, emotions sprout, but we know the great burden and responsibility that influences a global project, we know of the great importance , competitors are delivering much of their life and all their knowledge. Joharim is removed through the great bright tunnel, where no one wants to go, competitors continue their journey we meet the 8th month and this great competition is almost over, I recommend that you do everything possible to increase all your strengths, the efforts that are necessary, to transcend this great story, where we are all the main actors, I wish you the best, that you have wonderful days and a fantastic competitive continuity, that the last effort and encouragement will identify you.

Thank you great warriors for contributing to the great dream, follow your path with your head held high and your heart in your hand, you hear great applause the great ceremony is over, as I always retire, I go to my house to observe those great monitors that they have been a window into the unimaginable, those great stories, which complement life itself, are real stories, real emotions, real feelings, I saw Joharim, as a psychologist I observe the body language that they transmit before arriving with the great guru, semblant off, all the characteristics of a defeated being and the guru as if he had a magic wand, gives them the motivation they need, to continue on their great path.

Great guru I am here to show you my great pain, if daughter I listen to you what you have come to, tell what your heart feels and expresses, I feel defeated, I thought and I dreamed that I would be the winner, the daughter and all those who have They also deserved it, because they have simply delivered everything as if they were about to die and in a great competition as this is the most important and rewarding, your great 8 months of stay in this great place have given you a great treasure that you can express out there in the great world that awaits you, flourishing times await you, times to reap what you have sown, the only secret is that just as you fought in this place, in your daily life you must do it and when you can with more strength, identify every day in a different way, live every moment with strength, feel alive, fight for your dreams, when you least expect it, the grand prize of realization will come, your world awaits you with open arms, wants you to show is the great potential you have, the universe is witness to your achievements, your great spirituality, your discipline and commitment, you have an anchor that leads you to the creation of opportunities, take them you will be surprised, you have obtained in all this time a great treasure, part of your great wisdom, live great experiences to the fullest, cultivate the great moments, enjoy those harvests indicated for your life, thank you great guru, wonderful things happen in my mind, you have given me a great link to join my great chain made the realization, I feel calmer, your philosophy has enlightened me in all the senses, I know we have to keep in the great chest of our treasure, the great experiences lived, I have exchanged them for the precious wisdom, thanks guru, daughter sees the hand of being the best, your path is full of blessings, you have won a great legacy that the only thing you need is to develop it to the maximum with perseverance and dedication. I really watch Joharim with a great aura of light that surrounds his body, it is a special light that does not hurt the eyes, he retires like a great warrior, who gave life itself, I love how they retreat with great motivation.

It is time to see the great schedule that tomorrow will begin again in the great formation of our lives is the following;

Monday	Teacher	Subject
8:00 to 10:45	Salomomr	Special Forces Training Elite III
11:00 to 12:45	Laeva	Intrapersonal and interpersonal communication III

12:50 to 13:50   FOOD

14:00 to 15:45   Teslac   Global Strategic Mission III

16:00 to 17:45   McYuretzili Self-esteem and perception III

18:00 to 18:55   Edisonic Opportunities of transcendence III

19:00 to 20:00   Noetherli   Yoga universal III

Tuesday	**Teacher**	**Subject**

8:00 to 10:45   Salomomr Skills Growth and Training III

11:00 a 12:45   Markl   Globalized Social Intelligence III

12:50 to 13:50   FOOD

14:00 to 15:45   Vincir   Human strategic development III

16:00 to 17:45   Curielm   Integral Image Development III

18:00 to 18:55   Yessica Extrinsic and intrinsic motivation III

19:00 to 20:00   Noetherli   Yoga Universal III

Wednesday	**Teacher**	**Subject**

8:00 to 10:45   Yessica Extrinsic and intrinsic motivation III

11:00 to 12:45 Laeva   Intrapersonal and interpersonal communication III

12:50 to 13:50 FOOD

14:00 to 15:45   Teslac   Global Strategic Mission III

16:00 to 17:45   McYuretzili   Self-esteem and perception III

18:00 to 18:55   Edisonic   Opportunities of transcendence III

19:00 to 20:00   Noetherli   Yoga universal III

Thursday	Teacher	Subject
8:00 to 10:45	Salomomr	Skills Growth and Training III
11:00 a 12:45	Markl	Globalized Social Intelligence III
12:50 to 13:50 FOOD		
14:00 to 15:45	Vincir	Human strategic development III
16:00 to 17:45	Curielm	Integral Image Development III
18:00 to 18:55	Yessica	Extrinsic and intrinsic motivation III
19:00 to 20:00	Noetherli	Yoga Universal III

Friday	Teacher	Subject
8:00 to 10:45	Salomomr	Special Forces Training Elite III
11:00 a 12:45	Markl	Globalized Social Intelligence III
12:50 to 13:50	FOOD	
14:00 to 15:45	Vincir	Human strategic development III
16:00 to 17:45	Curielm	Integral Image Development III
18:00 to 18:55	Yessica	Extrinsic and intrinsic motivation III
19:00 to 20:00	Noetherli	Yoga Universal III

Saturday	Teacher	Subject
8:00 a.m. to 5:45 p.m.	Salomomr	Entrepeneur Deportivo de Elite III
	Yessica	
6:00 p.m. to 8:00 p.m.	Noetherli	Yoga Universal III

Sunday

Strategic rest; with work options according to the needs of the participant.

Important note:

All the subjects are focused, with the project of each competitor.

The large participation of competitors is extensive struggle with great energy, there are only four competitors, teachers are delivered as always in their classes to the fullest, they know that their great students have to be excellently prepared.

The big day arrives on the last Saturday of the ninth month, in a few minutes we will know who is the next competitor to retire, I notice the teachers a little nervous, but at the same time knowing that he is close to knowing who will be the big winner of this fantastic competition.

I am your Edisonic teacher, I am representing all the professors and collaborators of this great project, we have little time left, we are almost finishing this great adventure, it is for us a great happiness to belong to this great structure, in 3 days we have valued the great work of each one of you, our selection has been difficult, since everyone has special abilities that identify them, the leaders in the world, have used creativity and innovation as their main tools, today I thank the great leaders who have contributed to the great development of our large population, today in these times we have a great technology that we never imagined before, the great projects transcended personal difficulties, ridicule, lack of acceptance, where courage and courage arose in the face of these adversities. power of achievement that they obtained, it made these leaders transcend forever in history, they were you are the ones who dared to give, the heart, the soul, even sometimes life, so that their inventions were recognized.

That's why today I invite you never to give up in your life, that every day you see it as a different scenario, that you want great warriors who are willing to sacrifice their comfort zones, to achieve the most precious thing that is success, today we have met to know the great competitor who retires from this great stage, who retires is a great student who has transcended, if he continues on his way with the profile of a winner, what is present will achieve it, it is effective to mention that the great competitor that retires is, who showed a way of how battles can be won, his leadership will transcend like the great leaders, who gave up their life to get their way in the great story, the great person who retire today and remain forever in our hearts is;

5.- Name: Akeilas

Age: 34 years

Country: Russia

Profession: Doctor

Project: Health for everyone

Sport: Ice skating

Language: Russian, English, German, French

Altruism for the world: Physical and mental health to eradicate world poverty.

I know that for everyone it is a great privilege, to be in this majestic place, each one has written their own history, all have developed impressive behaviors, which makes them great leaders ready to everything, those are the leaders we need to govern the world , that the human sense characterizes them, what they think globally, in the needs of the world population and the most vulnerable, say goodbye to your great companion who gave everything for this great project, we all say goodbye, the hugs are stronger, we know that there are only 3 competitors left, who will be the worthy representatives, of all the competitors that have withdrawn, Akeilas retires, for that great tunnel full of light, you can see his face that was not on his part to remain in the group, He knows that I fight until the great end.

Competitors told them that only one month is needed in which you will be evaluated 3, to know who is the great winner, I invite you to continue striving, every day more, as the responsibility is increasing, the great moment is coming, I see the light From the sky, pointing to our surroundings, we can breathe a great air of triumph that all have been great participants, each competitor has put a great link to form the great chain that will support our great project, congratulations to the remaining competitors.

The great ceremony is over, with the novelty that in one month this competition ends and the stage of the development of the project begins, the great champion will have the facility, of exposing his great project before the world, only this coming month and we retire from this great place. I retire to my house, I urgently need to know what Akeilas thinks of this great occasion, I see her on the monitors is approaching the great temple of the guru, my daughter great competitor Akeilas, great guru, I have come to talk with you, I do not know how to start , daughter express yourself, I want you to say what you feel, great guru has been a great competition, I would like to see cattle, but it was not like that, but the great universe is witness to all my efforts to win, if daughter I know and I congratulate you , you are a great athlete, a great human being, a great competitor, this is the daughter in life, many times we are a second away from winning, I know you are understanding with the teachers, but for them the decision was also very complicated, I like it daughter, how you have taken things, your self-esteem is very high, you know that you have made countless sacrifices, that there is a rewarding world waiting for you that knows the great effort you have made.

Daughter what you just got today in this great scenario, from now on, is your personality, all this is already part of you, the power of your positive thoughts has reached you, with the great joy of being able to reach your goals with perseverance, discipline, efficiency, commitment, love daughter is already a fundamental part of you, you know what you have obtained, today in this day you are stronger, the energy has surpassed your great spirit, if great guru, I am very grateful for this great place has given me an infinity of experience and wisdom, that I can apply in any scenario that I am, daughter I believe in you, your words reach my heart, I know that you will never give up, that your struggle will be constant, that you know that you are a great warrior willing to surpass herself day by day. Thank you great guru for your motivating words, fill my heart and engrave in my mind, great warrior Akeilas, go with your head high satisfied with your great effort, the world awaits you with many options that will give you wealth to your life and your way, thank you great guru, they give each other a big hug, retire the great warrior who was in this wonderful scenario, I was surprised by his great mentality, he is a great human being, who deserved to win, but the reality is that all the competitors who left have deserved to win, this great stage has created the best leaders in the world, well it's time to rest tomorrow I expect a fabulous day.

It is Sunday, today I review the last schedule of the subjects, it is the following one;

Monday	**Teacher**	**Subject**
8:00 to 10:45	Salomomr	Transcendence of Elite
11:00 to 12:45	Laeva	Global Human Development
12:50 to 13:50 FOOD		
14:00 to 3:45	Teslac	Global Innovation
16:00 to 17:45	McYuretzili	Global Self-Realization
18:00 to 18:55	Edisonic	Creativity of transcendence
19:00 to 20:00	Noetherli	Spiritual Yoga

Tuesday	**Teacher**	**Subject**
8:00 to 10:45 Training	Salomomr	Sophisticated Elite
11:00 to 12:45 transcendence	Markl	World Intelligence of
12:50 to 13:50 FOOD		
14:00 to 15:45 Profile	Vincir	Development of a World
16:00 to 17:45	Curielm	Global Leadership

| 18:00 to 18:55 | Yessica | Braveness of the Leader |
| 19:00 to 20:00 | Noetherli | Spiritual Yoga |

Wednesday	**Teacher**	**Subject**
8:00 to 10:45	Yessica	Elite Training and Leadership
11:00 to 12:45	Laeva	Global Human Development
12:50 to 13:50	FOOD	
14:00 to 15:45	Teslac	Global Innovation
16:00 to 17:45	McYuretzili	Global Self-Realization
18:00 to 18:55	Edisonic	Creativity of transcendence
19:00 to 20:00	Noetherli	Spiritual Yoga

Thursday	**Teacher**	**Subject**
8:00 to 10:45	Salomomr	Sophisticated Elite Training
11:00 to 12:45	Markl	World Intelligence of transcendence
12:50 to 13:50	FOOD	
14:00 to 15:45	Vincir	Development of a World Profile
16:00 to 17:45	Curielm	Global Leadership
18:00 to 18:55	Yessica	Braveness of the Leader
19:00 to 20:00	Noetherli	Spiritual Yoga

Friday	**Teacher**	**Subject**
8:00 to 10:45	Salomomr	Transcendence of Elite
11:00 to 12:45	Markl	World Intelligence of transcendence
12:50 to 13:50 FOOD		
14:00 to 15:45	Vincir	Development of a World Profile
16:00 to 17:45	Curielm	Global Leadership
18:00 to 18:55	Yessica	Braveness of the Leader
19:00 to 20:00	Noetherli	Spiritual Yoga

Saturday	**Teacher**	**Subject**
8:00 a.m. to 5:45 p.m.	Salomomr Yessica	Elite Sports Leadership
6:00 p.m. to 8:00 p.m.	Noetherli	Spiritual Yoga

Sunday

Strategic rest; with work options according to the needs of the participant.

Important note:

All the subjects are focused, with the project of each competitor.

Classes begin, there is great motivation among the last 3 competitors, they fight day by day, with a huge energy, their leadership is identified why they are here, I know that no one will give up, perseverance is their faithful companion, Like the great professors are with more energy, they know that it is the last great effort, because their students are the best, I am amazed of the great subjects that are taking the competitors in this last month.

The third Saturday of the month arrives, we are in the great stadium, our great subject is Elite Sports Leadership, our great teachers are in front of us to give us the directions, Professor Salomomr speaks: great competitors, today is a great day, our group has decreased, we are 6 elite competitors willing to make our best effort, in the last big test of this course, it has given me great satisfaction to have a large group, the great feedback I have received from this great community of competitors , the great participants who retired left their imprint in this great place, but we are present today to make a story, a great story where our sweat, tears, pain was not an impediment to be champions, today we are willing to give life same as the challenges that this beautiful life proposes to us, our courage distinguishes us, our love strengthens us, we have the courage to fight r until the end, we know that our environment has 360 degrees, we are in the expectation of what happens, our spiritual control, our connection with the universe, today I will be able to deliver all the strength that is in me, adding the efforts that are necessary, today we will face a great test, which will give us a great profile to transcend, it depends on me if I want to cross the barriers of time, shortening them with the great goal of being a winner.

The helicopter will take us to the meeting point where we will do the big test, all are eager to know the challenge, but life will never tell you what is next, it will be matters of moments, of seconds, that you will know what you will face, there will be occasions that you make planning, but you must take into account that they are not always going to be perfect, like a manual that you can carry out when you want, life will give you tests that will make you kneel, fail, fall, but it depends on you you lift with more force, the predictable does not exist, but with work and dedication you can fulfill a prophecy of achievement, life is full of indescribable challenges, that make you grow, that make you value the times of happiness, of relaxation, of enjoyment , of joy, when the storm arrives, you must be willing to fight, waiting for the great battle, with determination.

Competitors join the helicopter an indecipherable path awaits us, a new battle to teach us that challenges give motivation, energy, strength, visualization, perspective, self-realization, the ability to feel alive, to know all the senses, to find spiritual power, we climb to the sophisticated helicopter, I have a little fear, I do not know what awaits us, what if it is that it is something very strong, in the professor's words you can see the weight of the challenge that awaits us, it is the last of these great challenges , I imagine that the teachers have to have done a great test where we remember them forever, I feel that my heart beats very strong, I will have to use the relaxation exercises that Professor Noetherli taught us, in spiritual yoga, after a moment, I feel better, this is great as each class is focused, self-realization, all the obstacles that arise in our day, it is efficient to look for solutions, all the teachers have fulfilled the great knowledge that they have transmitted to us, it has become wisdom, it is our treasure, our great toolbox ready to face the barriers that prevent us from continuing our journey, the professors notice them thoughtful, they know the great responsibility that It awaits them, they know that they have to exploit to the maximum the great potential that we have, we are arriving, the great helicopter goes down with a great softness, as if we were on a very cushioned carpet, we all go down, the professors are in front of us, competitors , I leave you with Professor Yessica, and then you will read an epitaph that contributes to personal improvement and says so;

In your mind, in your life, the most important thing is to win

Conformism does not exist.

Every day is a new day, in which you must deliver everything you have.

Think of your family, of your loved ones, who will observe in you.

Visualize yourself as a winner

Be aware of the sacrifices you will make to achieve the most precious thing is to be a winner.

In competitive matters, there is nothing more important than being the winner.

Your spirituality transcends the universe, when you are the winner, your brightness is reborn.

You have lost battles, but not war, your mentality is to win, think that miracles exist.

In your mind, in your life, the most important thing is to win.

Fight constantly, if things do not happen as expected, take perseverance afloat.

Your goal must always be present, losing the notion of time.

Day by day your armor has to be ready for the next battle.

When darkness invades your path, fight harder.

The light will be the biggest prize to your strength, the great breath to move forward with more strength.

Conformity, pretexts, irritability disappear from your life.

Enjoy every moment as if it were the last day you are in this beautiful world.

 In your mind, in your life, the most important thing is to win.

He sees each new challenge, as a new hope, as a new path full of learning.

Take the options that life gives you, as a great gift.

Dream, miracles exist and they give you surprises when you can not find an outlet.

Today I realized that the most important thing is to win.

When you are a winner, the clouds get shorter, there is a great connection with the universe.

When you are a winner the mountains reduce their size.

When you are a winner the obstacles fill you with energy, they give you power.

When you are a winner your spirituality grows.

When you are a winner, your senses are reborn, giving you a broader perspective of what is happening around you.

When you are a winner your legacy is ready, to enlighten future generations.

In your mind, in your life, the most important thing is to win.

Your commitment, must be tattooed in your mind and your heart, I will fight until the end to be a winner.

When fear disappears, courage gives you more peace of mind, to be a winner.

The universe is always going to witness your thoughts, your sensitivity, your emotions, your motivation.

Winning is my priority, winning is my base, winning is my spiritual platform towards realization.

There will be external factors that impede my achievements, with the internal factors I must fight them being positive, persevering, with the hunger to transcend.

My abilities are strengthened, I learn from failures, my falls do not prevent me from continuing.

I am aware that to transcend I must do extraordinary things.

I declare my commitment that the most important thing is to win.

Competing, anyone can do it, but winning is a small path, which the universe perceives.

I have the power to do my best, my victory motivates me to move forward.

My prize day by day will have given all the necessary efforts.

In your mind, in your life, the most important thing is to win.

Competitors is a great satisfaction and motivation to be with you before a big test, as the professor said life will be full of unpredictable obstacles, our manifestation must be aware, as we saw in the classes, we must manage a 360 degree conscious environment around us, the knowledge of what surrounds us is satisfactory to achieve our goals and objectives, competitors in 20 minutes we will perform the great test that consists;

1.-swim 10 kilometers in the sea

2.- To face the swell that is present with the acquired knowledge

3.- face the mental obstacles that impede the realization

We have to get to the other island that is reached to observe, we will receive the maximum protection of a modern and futuristic logistics team, the road will be indicated from the start of the departure, if they want to hydrate the nautical vehicles will provide what they need, it is a great test that will show us a natural, creative environment, it will be a great stage where our skills will be put to the test, in a few minutes the exit will be given, be alert.

What a great speech by the teacher, what a great motivation, what a great test awaits us, I see it as the maximum to do, I feel like another competitor, I know that I am the great observer, but it has been great to be involved with the competitors and The great effectiveness of the teachers, sounds a great shot that echoes in my ears, the adrenaline invades me, I am ready for the big challenge, we are a large group of 6 swimmers willing to transcend with this great test, which happens to me I am feeling a lot fear, the waves are very strong, I think I'm going to give up, no, I must reassure myself, if it were easy this great test anyone would do it, this is the maximum swim in the sea, before an unbreakable force, I will keep fighting and enjoying this great moment, thank God and reassure me, I am already at the end of these great tests, this great road, it is not fair to give up, where is the great philosophy that teachers have transmitted in each of their contributions and its great speeches, it is a great way we have a great technology that surrounds us, but the immensity of the sea controls us, I have never swum 10 kilometers, but it is a great test that awakens my senses, fills me with adrenaline, all the competitors and teachers are struggling against something unpredictable, as I continue my way a giant wave crosses my body and directs me in another direction, I think I'm getting lost, but I can observe the big island that is our objective, I hear a helicopter that Indicates that go to the right, I know that if I get to lose, I just swim to the island, the waves are impressive, since I left instead of decreasing, is increasing, the people who are responsible for logistics and we They are taking care of us, they can not see us, what helps them is the bracelet that indicates where we are, I am deviating from the place by swimming.

My God, help me, this is hell, the waves are tremendous, I am afraid that I will be attacked by an aquatic animal, they will locate me and tell me they will take me out of the test, due to the weather conditions, I tell them strongly, I'm never going to give up, it's an immense courage, let me continue, I know I can be prepared, they tell me that if I want to leave the competition I press the button that is on my wristband, if pressed it will emit frequency waves detected in seconds, touch the button, they never left me, I am alone with this majesty, knowing that only pressing a button would be in my comfort zone, not fighting anymore, that never, my goal, the island, gives me a great pleasure, that before the great swell, the island is observed, it is fabulous, but at the same time I feel fear, I do not know what I will find in this place, maybe a hungry shark, a stingray, I do not know, but messages are coming to my mind that they produce fear, re I agree with the great television conductor that a stingray with his sting pierced his heart, what a fear, but I have to continue with more force.

My God take care of me, I know that we only remember you when we have problems, but help me to achieve this great goal, I have lost the group I am alone in this place here in this immense sea, I am approached by a nautical vehicle indicating that if I am well and that I must swim more to the right, they tell me that there is a great building that is already observed, that this is my point of reference, I continue my way and I saw the building, but there are several, well I will continue swimming, what would happen with my group, they will be coming soon, I have lost track of time, I am swimming with an impressive force I urgently need to meet this goal, I will imagine that I am the winner, mitigate the fatigue, I am almost reaching the shore, I see several grandiose buildings with futuristic structures that adorn the island, a nautical vehicle approaches me, tells me to continue swimming to the right, that I already deviate a lot, that the building is majestic and shines like gold, that it continues like this Y that at any time I will observe it.

After an endless time and almost wanting to reach the shore, I see the big building, I'm almost there, I'm going to give my last strength, my waist hurts a lot, I'm going to relax to avoid the pain, my waist pain does not disappear, I'm going to think about the great goal and the prize that awaits me, it's a great break, I'm being escorted by several nautical vehicles to the finish, I feel more energized, I watch the beach, my eyes see the bottom better, I almost reach the shore of the beach, it was too long, but I will make the necessary efforts to achieve the goal, I'm about to stop, my eyes observe the great prize that is to reach the goal, I get up to run hard, but I fall, I continue I knelt down, I fall back, I fall back, what an effort, my God, but I'm already at the finish, I take a deep breath, I get up and run, crossed the finish line, this is great, my classmates had already arrived, I was the last one, What a disappointment but no way, for me it was a great gro having arrived after I got lost, yes, save my life, I am happy that I managed to cross the finish line, but my happiness would have been complete if I were the winner, in a few moments they would take out the lists of the winners and how the places were, They were waiting for me to arrive, check my wristband and tell me that the distance I traveled because I had lost was 11,357 meters. The great thing was that I made more than 10 kilometers that was the goal, what I did not like was that I lost, risked my life a lot, I am happy to have achieved my goal, but I would have liked to be the champion, winning is the most I can exist. So I leave the competition table;

1.- Professor Yessica

2.- Professor Salomomr

3.- Rosalinda

4.- Mahatmae

5.- Ryud

6.- Richc

The teacher won, what a great athlete she is, I never imagined that great result, the teachers ended up in the head of the great competition, that great and fantastic competition, I thought that I was not going to achieve it, the teacher addresses us embraces us, says, great competitors I am happy, we have achieved an extraordinary goal, despite the inclemency of our nature, this great goal was fulfilled, the teacher is crying, we all follow it is a great great goal that we have fulfilled, I Richc, save my life, I know I gave everything of me but I was not the winner, I have to keep working, because the most important thing is to win, we all express our emotions for the great goal achieved, the teacher tells us to breathe deeply, repeat with me this great prayer with the closed eyes;

Thank you great sea that you allowed us to cross.

Thank you great sea for allowing us to come alive to this great place.

Thank you great sea for letting us express how great you are.

 Thank you for giving us the opportunity to know a minimum part of your environment.

Thank you great sea, we recognize that it was not easy to be here.

Thank you great sea for making me transcend before the extraordinary.

Thank you great sea, it was spectacular, fantastic, our meeting.

Thank you great sea, for allowing me, to use my energies and my exhausting fatigue.

Thank you great sea for letting me live a great experience.

Thank you great sea because you let me find spirituality in this great crossroads.

Thank you great sea for giving me the opportunity to feel that the universe was with me.

Thank you great sea for the great journey that you allowed me to carry out.

Thank you great sea for letting me fulfill a dream more.

Thank you great sea, your power is unique.

Competitors have fulfilled a great goal that destiny made us, having options to surrender and not face a great obstacle that was presented to our lives in an unpredictable way, to face it was an experience that joined our wisdom, the universe is witness our transcendence, that we put aside our fears and resolved with courage our path that was presented with storms, the light illuminated the way, with the great hope of achieving our purpose. I leave you with Professor Yessica, it is for me young people an immense happiness to fulfill this great goal, where we are all alive, reliving illusions to continue our journey towards the pursuit of realization, we know that the important thing is to win, but sometimes there is battles that give us the happiness of only surviving, which is valuable to continue fighting, I know there are plenty of mixed feelings, but the priority is to get afloat, the maximum achievement that we have just made, we have fulfilled the maximum goal, our footprint and Transcendence will be recorded in the history itself, of our lives, the legacy we are building, the universe is witness to real life stories, which are willing to give everything to achieve the objectives and goals necessary to transcend. We enjoyed the great island, we were treated like true champions, our minds recorded in the story, a fantastic and spectacular situation that will never be erased, the great experiences are tattooed in the mind and the heart

Chapter VII

The last Saturday of the competition arrives, they are mixed feelings and at the same time nostalgic, because the great adventure is over, today we will know who is the great winner, after all this great time of knowledge directed towards wisdom and an extraordinary philosophy of life , we all know that the planned objectives have been met, we know that history is just beginning, the future winner has a great responsibility, that with his project the future generations, complement their lives with sense and happiness, their global project of the winner will be the matter prima to fill the corners that the world needs, we are 10 minutes to start the ceremony, all are nervous, teachers punctual in front of us, with the final notes of their great decision, it also depends on who will be the future leader with his project will give light to several lives in the world.

I am the teacher Yessica Sports Trainer Special Forces, it is 3 o'clock in the afternoon, today as everyone is a great day, but at the same time it is special because today we will know who is the great winner of this great competition, the teachers gathered, they know the great effort that has been spent to reach this great moment, where the great winner will represent us forever, our great organization, with altruistic world sense, all the competitors have been a great link, so that the chain of the great project, come out strong before humanity, all have been excellent competitors, who have given our lives a great sense of belonging, it is for me great and satisfying to mention at this time to the third place, is a great competitor, that I fight day with day, storm after storm, his philosophy was to win, but the evaluations are necessary for the transcendence of the objectives, the great competitor that is going is, a person who showed that the motivation It can arise from unimaginable places, that his faith and hope led him to this great place, he is a great warrior who won countless battles, but today we have to say that the competitor that retires is, the person who handled his emotions with sincerity , who knew that being here required courage, perseverance, love for what he was doing, the great competitor that retires is the number;

12.- Name: Ryud

   Age: 27 years

   Country: Japan

   Profession: Electronics Engineer

   Project: Harnessing solar energy

   Sport: Karate

   Language: Japanese, English, German

Altruism for the world: Use solar energy to eliminate poverty in the world, transport with solar energy, electricity, food.

His great project is motivating, but the road continues, leave him with a strong and great applause, everyone says goodbye to him, with tears in his eyes, addresses all the teachers giving them thanks and a big hug, retires Ryud, through the big tunnel, it is the third place in this competition.

We continue this situation is difficult, but our good cause deserves the great sacrifices, all the competitors that have passed through this great place, its imprint is recorded, it is magnificent to appreciate each one of the skills and strengths, that exemplified each competitor, before continue with the departure of the last competitor, I want you to watch this great video, 30 minutes of a compilation of all the competitors, with their teachers, it is great to observe these great life stories that were lived in this great place, we started, we observed the video that was edited brilliantly, shows each competitor's personality and his stay short of what characterized him, we were all amazed with the video, they all showed their emotional side with tears, nobody wants to leave, it's great how this project is done with great love

The big party continues the second place will be for a great person who manifested his greatness through the facts, his great sensitivity taught us, that the priority of teamwork had to be done always, that the constant practice, took awards that they could enjoy the day-to-day satisfaction of having delivered the maximum effort in each activity they performed, the competitor that retires is a great example to follow, also worthy of the first place, but we know that in the great responsibilities they must make sacrifices, the great competitor that retires is, a great person that transcended, with a 360 degree approach, it is magnificent and fantastic to live with this great leader, his leadership is exemplary, his successes sound like achievement bells in the face of storms , the great competitor that retires is, a person with great motivation, with great perseverance, with great control, with great spirituality and with a great connection with the universe, the great competitor that retires is the number;

2.- Name: Rosalinda

Age: 32 years

Country: MEXICO

Profession: Food Engineer

Project: Nourishing food for the world

Sport: Swimming

Language: Spanish, English, Japanese

Altruism for the world: create your own foods that are nutritious and enjoyable.

Everyone says goodbye to her, but Rosalinda will be with Ryud and the winner at the awards ceremony. You already imagine who is the great winner, he is a great warrior, our worthy representative, the great responsibility that awaits him is important, but we know that the great mission project, to eliminate world poverty, is in good hands, he showed us during his stay here as the projects must be carried out with dedication, love, perseverance, spirituality, we are grandly proud of you the winner is;

11.-Name: Mahatmae

Age: 24 years

India country

Profession: Mathematical physicist

Project: lend money for creation of businesses that give employment

Sport: Yoga

Language: Hindi, English, Spanish, French, Italian, Russian, Chinese

Altruism for the world: Use creativity and innovation to encourage the population in the world to create their own jobs by providing financing to projects that have a future.

It is a splendid celebration, artificial games, confetti, everything that brings a great party, all teachers are happy to have selected the great winner, the award ceremony begins, the podium is waiting for the finalists and the big winner, it comes out from under the floor playing an orchestra, which fills the ears with great sensations, it is a hymn to triumph, to relaxation, to rest, because it almost ends today, but the symphonies motivate that the work is not over, that we are starting, a lady comes out on a movable stage, which is on the side of the orchestra begins to sing;

The triumph, fill our hearts

Tears have disappeared, tranquility has arrived.

I never imagined the result, but I always tried my best.

full bliss came to me I have achieved the most success.

But I know it's not over yet, my direction, my direction.

I have to keep working, I have to keep fighting.

My love is so great for what I do, my happiness grew day by day.

I have won a great battle, but it continues a great way, to be solved.

For me these are the beginnings, a sigh to my life, a prize of encouragement.

Life goes on, time does not stop, I am happy and I enjoy today.

Tomorrow I do not know, if I will feel this great happiness again.

The passion invades me, my energy returns, my love invades.

The universe, the universe, the universe, the universe was the only witness.

Miracles exist came to my life beginning with a dream.

My love is so great for what I do, my happiness grew day by day.

I have won a great battle, but it continues a great way, to be solved.

For me these are the beginnings, a sigh to my life, a prize of encouragement.

Life goes on, time does not stop, I am happy and I enjoy today.

Tomorrow I do not know, if I will feel this great happiness again.

What I do know is that I must love with all my strength.

That every day I must live it to the fullest, as if I were going to die.

Dying to live, dying to live, dying ... to ... Live.

What a fantastic song shows the human side of achievement, transcendence, each note is spiritual, each note has a universal connection, we continue with the ceremony, at this moment there will be awards and recognition to the third place Ryud, these are the prizes that you will receive;

1.- A scholarship in the best school in the world.

2.- A group in charge of master minds to carry out your project.

3. - A trip for all the people, that you want that they go with you, during a month to the place of the world that they want.

4.- Prize in cash.

5.- Recognition and Bronze medal.

For the great second place Rosalinda these are the great prizes that you will receive;

1.- A scholarship in the best school in the world.

2.- A group in charge of master minds to carry out your project.

3.- A trip for all the people, that you wish that they go with you, during a month to the place of the world that they want.

4.- Prize in cash.

5.- Make yourself a dream you want, reality.

6.- Recognition and Silver medal.

For the very first place, the great winner Mahatmae the prize is;

1.- Carry out your project worldwide.

2.- We will provide you with the best group of world masterminds, to carry out the project.

3.- A trip for all the people that you want to go with you, during two months to the place of the world that they want.

4.- Prize in cash.

5.- Make two dreams that you want, reality.

6.- Recognition and Gold medal.

The grand ceremony is over, the winners are on the podium, the ritual is similar to the greatest competition in the existing world, the winners take countless photos, the face of happiness they have is something unique is a great relief, teachers are join the party is happy, they know that the work continues, but that the bases are already formed of the great structure that is thought to form, all competitors receive a memorandum from the great guru Taoci, where are the schedules that will receive them, is a great farewell, finishing talking with him, the second and third place of the island is removed, the great winner will retire the next day, in the memorandum, the schedules were as follows;

1.- Ryud 17:30 temple of the great guru

2.- Rosalinda 18:30 temple of the great guru

3.- Mahatmae 19:30 temple of the great guru

I'm already in the monitors waiting for the third place Ryud who will talk with the guru Taoci, it's 5:25 PM, he's already arriving at the temple, great guru, son was waiting for you, thank you great guru, my greatest wish was win and I could almost assure you, if your son is really a great competitor, full of intelligence, today you leave with a lot of wisdom, I know him as a great guru, the page of my past has been closed, my profile today is different, I have another mentality, I decide to stay with this, I congratulate you son you have matured very fast, your stay in this great place has been enriching, your strengths have grown, your spirituality has transcended, your manifestation towards the universe gives off a light that is in constant communication, son you are a great human being, who will always enjoy great success, as you see life, it is what belongs to you, your positive thoughts have generalized your mind, a thought that makes you universal, your leadership will be fruitful or, wherever you are, your manifestation will be taken into account as you meet the great essential characteristics of a great leader, you will find on your way an infinity of people proud of you, of your achievements, of your innovative and futuristic advances, but with the main basis of living the present to the fullest.

Great guru I am going to miss this great place, I know son this is an earthly paradise, but this you lived can be conceived outside, I know that today you do not think about riches, you know that the only thing that is base in this life, for great structures is happiness, you realize son, you have never sought riches, you have always liked to make the most effort, but you know that wealth is abundant around you, son continues your way with strength, you have grown your strengths, you have still side your weaknesses, your footprints will be constant, your path will have obstacles but it will be full of abundance, your family will have a recognition to your person, that will transcend for generations, human development will be your priority, you will surround yourself with committed individuals, to look for the success, cultivating excellence, son go with God and enlighten the universe, thank you very much guru, it was fantastic for me to talk with you, your wisdom has transported me, I thank you for your I hear what I have obtained in this place along with your knowledge, I am more spiritual, I know that I belong to the great universe, they say goodbye with a big hug, the monitors see a great aura of energy that surrounds them.

What magnificent words of the great guru, cultivate in you the knowledge, positive thoughts, perseverance, love, universal spirituality, a few minutes before 18:30, I am waiting for the competitor who obtained the second place Rosalinda, I already observe her in the monitors, you almost reach the great temple, you hear the voice of the guru, daughter ahead tell me I hear you, great guru I'm a little pensive, my question because I did not get the first place, I felt very capable of being the winner, you are a daughter since you came to this great place you were considered a winner, now that you leave with greater reason, I see you as a great winner, who had all his tools to make his dream come true, all the time you manifested with your facts to which you came and was to win, you are a great woman who will transcend forever.

Great guru but I do not have the first place, daughter as teachers have said in this life they have to make sacrifices and many times they are, you are for me a great champion, you did not win, but you were about to win, you surrender total each day, manifest your universal connection, you are a great leader, an example to follow, the ease with which you handle challenges make you special, what if I tell you what you propose in your mind is realizable, you know that dreams they come true and you know that miracles exist, daughter always walks with her head held high, with your 360 degree perception, that you know that when you see the outside you complement your life, if you work with enthusiasm inside you become stronger, you have a profile security, because you know who you are since you have come to this wonderful world, I invite you to be as you are, always fighting each day with greater strength, there are many goals that await you out there, with the initiative to start any er project, a great treasure, is that the fear of your mind has disappeared, you have found synchronization, how to carry out your plans, you have a wonderful potential, which gives you the gift of turning dreams into reality.

Thank you great guru for your support, for your great words, for your wisdom, daughter sees with God and with the great illusion of achieving what you please, with perseverance, dedication and love, they embrace a shining aura envelops them. I will miss his words of the great guru, the advice and interventions that reflect his greatness, the great champion is coming to arrive at 7:25 pm, I already see him on the monitors the great champion Mahatmae, son forward, great champion forward, thank you great guru, I come to thank you for your great advice that made me a more human, more spiritual person, son I am here to help you when necessary, I admire you son, you took out all your potential, all your tools, all your strengths, that you imagined that they did not exist, if a great guru, this spiritual place has served to find myself, forever for my mind, to win and be the maximum representative of this great place, of this great project, if son I am pleased you know the responsibility that you have in your being, you are a great man, that has always fought, today you know that you have to fight harder, because you are a great leader that represents a great community, that represents the world, t your global thoughts, I direct you to your spirituality that stands out and your universal ideas, son enjoy these great moments, enjoy with your family, your loved ones, for when you join to apply the project you are ready, great guru I feel with so much enthusiasm that I am able to follow and not rest, I know you have a magnificent energy that characterizes you, but it is important that you take a break so that you arrive with more strength, ready to give everything, willing if you are to die to live.

If son when we finish a goal and like you with a great triumph it is important to celebrate, since it was not easy to be here among great competitors, your learning is full, you must always have it in constant practice, your transcendence is real, sophisticated, futuristic, thanks great guru I love your great words, son is something that corresponds to you were the winner, I recognize your work, your conscience, your connection with the universe, thank you great guru, I had problems in the past, but today my scars have disappeared , I have become a human being who values what surrounds him, if your universal sense son, belongs to the great leaders, you inherited that spiritual strength connects you with the universe, son is always how you are, you do not need to change anything about you , you know that today you have to fight harder, because tomorrow is uncertain and the past you know that you should only consult the good, be positive that your heart be filled with the aura of happiness, ue full life, smiles, the full enjoyment of what you do, give meaning to your life, always look for your accessories, take advantage of all the options that you of life, life is unique, the times are often unrepeatable, love with strength, enjoy love to the fullest, your spiritual encounters with the universe, you know that miracles exist and that everything starts with a dream, that when you least expect it can become reality, if great guru and thank you very much this was a great dream come true, a great miracle never imagined, I expect a great job, I know that in these great moments I will only enjoy what I have with all my senses.

Son go with God, with great strength, great courage, today son to finish this great story, but start a new one, you are the great winner of this great project Mission, eliminate world poverty, belong to the world global technologies will be faithful companions, united to the masterminds that are in your charge, your life is full of meaning, you will illuminate many hearts around the world, thank you great guru for your support, I need your blessings to continue my great journey towards the realization of a great world that has what is necessary to be happy, that everyone feels proud that their most basic expectations are fulfilled, son I bless you in the name of the great project, all those who formed the great organization where you took your first steps will be blessed forever, you have already started son a series of steps that have created the bases, for the great structure that will form around the world. They embrace the light shines like the sun, the good intentions light up any heart, a great job awaits the great winner Mahatmae, the greatest miracle of having the winner was fulfilled, now, we have to continue dreaming so that the miracle is achieved more great of all the history in the world "Mission, eliminate world poverty".

There is a global call, where committed leaders are sought, with solutions to existing problems, in the innovation profile, creativity plays a very important role being the main basis of any structure that you want to build. The challenges in the globalized world, demand efficiency, perseverance, humanity.

The transformation of the world in a positive way requires a lot of work and courage, to face the challenges that are day by day, they are great obstacles that impede the realization, the leader must adapt with the tools that counts, leaving aside the pretexts or fundamentals unfounded that prevent realization.

The leader of today must have the courage to emerge from where nobody imagines, where everyone gave up on the project, that's where the great warriors have to face the battle that comes along, with the great vision of finding the transformation towards the realization , the approach manifests daring to invent to create ideas that make a better world, where future generations have been observers with the premise that dreams come true, that the positive proposals that are carried out, count for a better way of life.

Technologies are a great tool that facilitates communications, streamlines the exchange of ideas, for the realization of specific objectives in terms of time, short, medium and long term goals, these days has a greater projection towards success, with their degrees of difficulty, the barriers that simplify the achievements, must be broken with the great dream of a change that benefits the populations, the communities in the world, seek fruitful examples of teaching, to apply them in their organizations.

The hunger for knowledge exists in the world, leaders must demonstrate by example, that every objective can have results with great dedication, love towards projects shows enthusiasm, the great energy that is needed in times of crisis, the motivation that comes in times of storms, is necessary for the realization, large projects focused on humanity, acquire a great added value, which are always manifested in societies.

The failures can be great barriers that impede our path, but it is necessary to begin to face any challenge that comes up, with great courage in the present, freeing all the senses to be in expectation of what awaits us for the great conviction and dare to want to change our life story, be willing to face what is presented is a great armor before the storms and adversities "In the failures is not all pain, they leave you great experiences of how things should not be done " the magnificent of life is the great learning that the practice leaves you, it is a great reality when you are working to achieve your goals, it will not be an easy way everything in this life has its degree of difficulty, it depends on how you are willing to take that great challenge

"The road to success, is not as far as we think, it will be shorter if we focus our mind on achieving it; with effort, struggle and determination", achieving success is not easy, but if you got it without difficulty, what value would you give it, when battles, you fight constantly and the realization of the project does not arrive, the desperation visits you, you constantly ask and you balance everything the weight of what you have done, of what you have sacrificed to be there in search of your goal, your valorization is sometimes cruel it fills you with bitterness, knowing that you have not achieved your priorities, but when the great light comes to your life that is success, is that great glass of water that you receive in the desert, that great prize that you will value forever, success has great degrees of difficulty, but keep in mind forever, that it is worth the great sacrifice.

"The seed you sow, will depend on you if it withers or grows ", start your project with strength, dream, stay focused, make your realization part of yourself, your great intentions will accompany you forever, think positive, but with a great job and perseverance, it opens the doors to great achievement, the manifestation focused on the great moment that belongs to you, which is the great present, it will be a necessary base to determine, the steps that will lead you to reap that great prized fruit, that you created willing to give life itself, to receive the great trophy to the realization of what you started, that product that identifies you and focuses you to receive the maximum prize, the fruit that was born among the storms.

" On your way to success there will be someone who criticizes you, questions or mocks you, but perhaps this person already tried. The world is of enthusiastic people, who struggle daily to differentiate themselves, from those who do not dare and who have a positive mind, from a winner ". Make up your mind today is the great day, today begins with strength, determination, enthusiasm, to change the world around you, the main thing is that you start with you, you are the owner of your thoughts, you have the ability to be better every day, give the great example, that you dared to begin before the uncertainty, before the storms, before the pain, the place of comfort has disappeared in you, you are willing to fight like a great warrior to achieve your great dream, your decision is an important factor for start, mentalize day by day, observe your goal and capitalize what you are willing to do to make your dream come true.

"The sport is the essence of the spirit and the constant struggle, towards the mentality of the future", in times of stress, conflicts, lack of initiative, sport is a great motivation tool, the neurotransmitters that you release when you do a sport activity, they give you an enthusiastic mentality before the challenges that arise, taking the initiative before the obstacles requires a lot of effort, the sport keeps you relaxed and aware of what you have to contribute to make your dreams come true, when you practice a sport with discipline, focus, perseverance, begins to enter your life a healthy mind, with the premise that everything you propose will have its degrees of difficulty, you are a great warrior willing to deliver the efforts that are necessary to get your big project Make reality, you have to pay the price of getting the dream you want.

"We are the only species that thinks, if this mentality is positive, everything that we propose we will achieve with effort and dedication. You have to make the maximum effort in the place that belongs to you, because in most of the times the future is uncertain", it is difficult to predict the future, today, it is the great scenario that belongs to you, use all your tools, all your experience, the great challenge will require all your potential, the past was a great treasure, take the best, what will serve you for the present battle, prepare yourself with courage, your road to success, it will have darkness, storms, do not be afraid, continue your path more strongly, tears will visit your face, pain will be present, but when the great miracle comes, knock on your door, welcome it with immensity, enthusiasm and love, it is the great success that you hoped for forever, enjoy its flavor, thank of heart the fantastic moment.

"We have to dare to reach where many fear, where there are problems, where we feel we can not, there is success", in our great way there are difficulties, sometimes they are so powerful that they impede our path, it even makes it difficult for us wake up from catastrophes, think forever because you are in this wonderful world, to be the best, the concept is difficult, but when you fight with a huge force, without waiting for a prize, you focus on the result of the time lapse that belongs to you , in the great present, think forever, every day is different, every day requires your greatest effort, when sweat runs through your body, when fatigue makes you weak, is that today you fought with strength and determination, when your effort is sincere, the great universe listens to your determination, to want to change positively in 360 degrees, all around you is illuminated with great strength, that you are willing to surrender to the great challenge or with everything you say, your vision is focused on the great moment, you know that at any unexpected moment you will begin to observe the great results that your great spirituality has given you.

"A book without underlining what is important to you, it is as if you had not read it," it is important that you document, that you receive all the information that contributes to your internal and external growth. In the world the information runs in seconds, the learning of yesterday, today may have changed, we have infinity of information that the technologies provide us, it depends on us to select the great information that facilitates our lives, that fills us with knowledge . It is important to have constant hunger for learning, to enrich knowledge, they are a great foundation for the structure of life, constantly read, analyze the world around you, meet the brilliant minds of all times, have a varied menu of information, in where you only have to select the one that you like, the one that you know will complement your development tools.

"What you think you are, is your projection of who you are, if you think you are a failure, that you are defeated, it is true, if you think the opposite that you are positive, successful, a great winner, that is what you are", your great mentality treats you as you treat it, your thoughts about you are what you project in your life, if you have had a lot of problems, your sense of existence has many conflicts, begins to analyze cases, looks for people with more problems than you, observes how confront them, analyze the life stories of the brilliant minds of all times, most had countless conflicts, worse than yours, emerged from nothing, emerged from where there was no exit, emerged from where many fell defeated, looking for stories of life that motivate you to keep going, receive positive information that teaches you how to emerge from nowhere, how to get up in the face of storms, before storms, focus on being better every day, you are unique you are unique In life there is no other person like you, you will find some characteristics or similar features, but never another person like you.

¨ You are like a firefly you transmit light, do not let evil influences and envy extinguish that brightness ¨, love, love, appreciate, count on a magnificent machine, never comparable, it is your great body that belongs to you, uses all your senses to appreciate what surrounds you, be more spiritual, complement your great life being positive, select very well the people around you, you own your space, positive friendships contribute to your development, avoid problematic friendships at all costs, enjoy life to the fullest, living your days with great happiness, with a sincere love, you are a fantastic firefly, do not let your light go out, that positivity enters your life, stay forever in your heart, comments that are as obstacles, give them back, avoid them to the fullest, you are in this great world to live in the best way, appreciate the true feelings, focus on the true emotions, your concept of life has to transcend and be a worthy example of the great capacity you have to live to the fullest, your life is unique, you are the great actor who has to be able to strive on the great stage that belongs to the great present.

¨ Success is in your hands, you just have to look for it; with constant struggle, perseverance, dedication, effort and courage¨, your great goal must be embodied in your mind, that dream that motivates you to continue facing the defeats, storms, adversities, decide today to start, what you achieve, however minimal it may be celebrate it, feel the great satisfaction of gratitude, that runs through your veins. You are a new person, you know that your purposes can become reality, but when you feel the opposite, that there is no way out, that you are destroyed, that your body has a great burden that does not allow you to continue, that obstacles have stopped you, analyze things to the fullest, what you are looking for will not be easy to achieve, but if the great miracle comes full of light, receive it with all your abilities, have in your mind recorded that miracles exist, that in the storms an immense light can arise, to change your stormy days, decide, today is the great stage that belongs to you.

"By knowing the emotions that cause you pain, you become stronger", painful emotions affect our lives, affect our achievements, affect our great path, but nobody in the world is immune to pain, all at a certain time, we will face the great challenge of attacking the emotions that affect us, it is difficult to talk about these situations, but it is real life, sometimes the pain can make us stronger or it may be the opposite to impede our path, there are infinite suffering in our lives that defeats us, that sometimes makes the great sense of our lives disappear, mentalize yourself, those emotions at any time you will live them or if you are living them, do not feel fear the only sophisticated weapon against suffering is to live it to the fullest, to be forever spiritual, cry, feel that pain that consumes you, express it do not feel fear, time will witness the great obstacle that prevents you from being happy, the great universe in which Any moment will make you the great miracle of healing your wounds or diminishing them, you are a great warrior, who will emerge with a huge force of that great pain, sometimes you will lose countless battles, but be aware that you have not lost the war, If you are in this wonderful world it is for something.

¨ When someone motivates you, you can perform challenges you have never imagined. Love breaks all stereotypes¨, motivation is very important in our lives, look for it constantly, get it from people, characters, books, examples of life stories, from someone you admire, from any positive place that comes your way, smart to select the great information, which will serve as a great tool to emerge from the unforeseen, motivation is a great essence to meet our goals with decision, when there is someone around you or something that motivates you is a great treasure that you should appreciate With all your strength, this great treasure is one of the best fuels in the world, to face any challenge that comes your way, spirituality is a great connection with the universe, when sincerity invades your heart, your world changes from the inside to the outside, true love complements your life, if you have this great emotion so precious, your life is complete and if you do not relax, enjoy what surrounds you the most , in any situation that you use your senses, the great emotion will appear where you least expect it, enjoy to the maximum the things that sometimes are called simple or without value, they can give you the great surprise that they are part of your life and lead you to a positive determination that will help you achieve your goals.

"Human value is a factor of global development", when you value the people around you, accept their strengths and weaknesses as any great human being, human value is a great factor of development for all successful organizations in the world , where human beings feel happy, where they do the work they are in love with, where they accept challenges, where solutions are given, where they innovate, where creativity exists, that's where the best development approach appears . Make a decision to be better every day, in the place where you are, the greatest effort is that which identifies your great profile, human value is a factor of global development, people committed to development projects, maintain a synergy with the brilliant minds, each approach that is carried out, with sincerity, with great effort and perseverance, is able to emerge from the same ashes, from where nobody imagined, from where infinity of thoughts came up with the conclusion that only a miracle could give the solution , put on the shirt of your organization, you are unique in life and you are capable of giving life itself to transcend before the storms, before the great obstacles, before the great adversities.

"All work has a meaning, a way of living", what you propose you will achieve with hard work, your perseverance focus, will give the expected results, "Pear the best to life, but be aware of what you are willing to offer to achieve that great dream longed for, that great divine miracle that is the realization of your goals, projects, a great way of living, our lives are unique, countless experiences will never be repeated again, live your time lapses to the maximum, today is a great day to use all your skills, to enjoy the great pride of having done your work to the maximum effort, you do not have to give anything to anyone of your positive acts, just take them out with a great responsibility and decision , without waiting for results, without waiting for rewards, the great universe will detect your thoughts, your wonderful mentality, when you least imagine it, the big rewards will knock on your door, with that light that illuminate even your big heart.

Follow the best examples that life provides you, analyze the exemplary life stories that draw your attention, surround yourself with positive learning, the great knowledge that complements your life, fight with a huge force to be better every day, you are the actress or the main actor of your life, you have the free will to join the idea that pleases you, you have the free will to make the decision that is effective for you, that your body is surrounded by light, changes the results if they are not the expected ones , have the courage to start today, with the great determination to change in 360 degrees, your great changes you will notice in the short, medium or long term, do not look for a lapse of time, just start, dream, start to believe that there is a great spiritual force that has moved all the bright minds of our times, the past has witnessed that great power, decide today to change to be a better person for you, for the beings that surround you, for the societies, for your culture, for the world, today is the great moment to demonstrate why you are in this wonderful land, accept the challenge that presents itself, however difficult it may be, you have to find the solution alternatives, your capacities will increase, because you saw the courage to accept the great challenge that infinity of people did not dare.

Get dressed, use that great armor that you have rusted and stored, for when you decide to start, throw the fears into the trash, throw away the pretexts, better live to the fullest, no matter how hard, all the battles that you dare to face even if you are not a winner, they will leave you an apprenticeship, however minimal it may be, they will invite you to the path of experience, your job is to accumulate all this learning, so that in time you start visiting the great lands of wisdom, when you dare infinity of benefits that being crossed arms, in your comfort zone, will not appear by magic, be aware that everything you want in this life can be yours, but you must be willing to pay the great price, renew your energies day with day being spiritual, there is an unknown force that listens to your surrender, that reads your thoughts, fills your mind with the best, lives to the fullest what the path gives you, do not despair, relax, practice a sport, so that your frustrations come out, your mind must be kept clean, it must be ready to face the challenge that presents itself, your weapons must be ready for whatever comes, never expect the best scenario, look forward to the unpredictable, willing to to fight and to dream to obtain the great miracle of which the light arrives at your great scene, when you feel that you can not look at your objective, visualize yourself with force and observe that they are worth the sacrifices.

Faith, a great priceless treasure, is needed in times of crisis or in hard work, to achieve the desired goal, the world needs a great faith focus towards overcoming. The creation of projects facilitates a dynamic interior and exterior, the combination of different ideas towards the solution of problems, the intervention of different actors of society, facilitates a great synergy, where the results can be seen in short periods of time, the desire, the motivation towards creation and innovation, is the essential premise for the development of prototypes, which benefit societies in the world. Make constant calls, to find committed, enthusiastic, perseverant leaders, brilliant minds that are willing to develop in any environment, with the right solutions for a global contribution.

Decision to start; fill yourself with courage, begin, accept the challenge, focus on the great challenge that awaits you, today will be a different day, because you have decided to change your inner profile in 360 degrees, start with the great desire to deliver all your energy, your enthusiasm , your courage, in the great goal you desire with great desire, dream has no cost, it is free to visualize your goal, what if it will cost you, it will be a great investment, reach success, analyze forever if what you want is not it costs you, you would never appreciate it, when you deposit all your efforts, that at the end of your day you feel faint, you are ready for the next stage, the universe will be a great observer of your total surrender, of your desires of change, of your desires of overcoming. If suffering invades you, you find no way out, you want to give up, analyze to what you have come to this great world, you are here to be better every day, accept the challenge, when you achieve the precious achievement you will enjoy it with strength, but you will be with the condition of waiting for the next challenge.

Know your body, enjoy your senses that are your property, the great spiritual manifestation invades your mind, the world is complex. Wake up you are a unique and special being, face your weaknesses, develop your strengths every day, are your tools that identify you with your environment, you are alive, feel the air that caresses your body, look for that pleasant smell that impacts your senses, observe what you want, enjoy what you want, the transcendence of your spirit belongs to you, you are in this wonderful world, with the simple fact of being happy, clear mind that opens up sufferings, not everything in life is sweetness, but those storms you do not you create them, they manifest themselves in unpredictable moments, which sometimes prevent you from continuing, listen to the sounds you like, when the obstacles are presented, your tools are available, to search for light, sensitivity makes you receptive to any feeling, value that you give, will be a part of the architecture of your life.

You are a creative being show it, in the world there are countless types of intelligence, you are intelligent, look where you are a good warrior or where you wish to be, you have a great capacity for decision, you have the great privilege of choosing what you want, including the challenge what you want to face, is your great responsibility, focus on your desires, where you are willing to give life itself, be receptive to what surrounds you, when you least expect it you will notice the great exterior that belongs to you. Join the pieces of your creation, go without desperation forming your great bases, your structure, dream of the great moment of observation, towards your great construction, that work of art that identifies all your achievement, all that you were able to offer to achieve your fantastic goal, begins today with a huge strength, that you yourself astonish, when you detect that great energy that facilitates your path, go with a slow, but firm step towards your life project.

"Wake up, today is the great day to start, in the wonderful present", constantly in our journey of realization, we are presented with barriers, obstacles, that sometimes prevent us from continuing, fill us with great fear, which we constantly express when we try change our mentality, to positive thoughts, even sometimes stop our way with such force, we find no way out, we know in advance that on countless occasions only a miracle can save us. It is very important to be spiritual, in what you create you must sensitize yourself and make a connection in a sincere way where your feelings are a great light in union with the universe. If you have gone through many storms or are currently experiencing problems where the solutions do not arrive, you keep fighting with more force, all that pain transports you with courage to your energy, with a great courage to want to change positively, fight with strength, you have the right to happiness.

The suffering on countless occasions defeat us makes our paths are complicated, it is a great weight that is in our body, it prevents us from walking with strength and decision, everyone in this life is exposed to suffering to a greater or lesser degree, but it manifests or appears in some quadrant of our lives.

The analysis, the value, the great experience that life gives you on a day-to-day basis, examining life stories compared to what you are living, is a great approach to develop strengths in storms, nobody is immune to pain, but you are owner of your feelings, your actions, you have the free will to solve problems, when you can not find an exit, get up off the ground, start again, walk, if you can not crawl, remember the learning you got when you were little , all those great blows that made you mature, that great learning that you got from all those falls, do not despair the important thing is to be centered in the manifestations of your feelings, when you express what you feel no matter how hard you are, through time the great miracle where those emotions that affected you day by day diminish, not in their totality, but they are great manifestations, that help you to continue fighting, you begin to feel like the energy runs through your body, giving you the great tools necessary to face what is presented.

It starts again, it is hard when you feel that you almost reach the top and suddenly you have to start over again, it is very hard and frustrating, but sometimes it happens in our lives, but we must value when we achieve the great achievement of the goal , there comes a moment of calm, our heart manifests a powerful energy, which keeps us active and willing to face the next challenge, but in this life is easy, everything that we propose has its degrees of difficulty, when you fight day by day and you maintain your positive mentality, you are close to your goal, your focus must manifest an acceptance to the challenges, because only with them will you achieve an active life where the sense towards what is presented to you is manifested in the enjoyment of the time lapse it belongs to you in the great present.

Dream of your goal, the great world characters of our history began their life project with an image, a great visualization that became a dream, with hard work, focus, perseverance, determination, suffering, it became the great dream reality, that I contribute to world development, innovation, creativity, great ideas, you start with a dream, with time it becomes a miracle come true. What are you willing to offer for your great dream, countless characters of history have offered for their great achievement, even their lives, of course it is a concept of individual character, it is not necessary to give your life, because you would not enjoy your great success, What if you must develop, are your skills to the maximum and focus on your goal, when you feel faint for the great effort, is that you are near your realization.

There are countless occasions in our lives, we are about to give up, unconsciously we decide to continue and what is the great surprise that we achieve our great goal, our in-depth analysis comes where we ask ourselves. Was I already about to give up? If I had given up, I would not have succeeded ?, they are great moments where we observe the great magic of continuing to fight forever. The great miracles that are presented to us in life, many times we do not perceive them until they occur. When we do not find an exit, when we feel that we have already done everything necessary to achieve our goal and the results do not appear, in that great darkness there appears a bright light, which is the marvelous miracle. Miracles exist, but for them to occur, you must analyze what you are willing to offer, ask for the best in life, but with the balance of what you will give of your part, be positive, but every day observe it differently, the great effort that You performed in yesterday to stay in the past, you are in the magnificent present, you are a great warrior, with the mentality and strength to face a new battle.

You are a great actor, who is on a great stage that is your life itself, the script you handle, you have the free will to do what you please, do it with a great responsibility, leave your mark in this world that the great universe I recognized you, because you always fought, you cried, you suffered, you persevered, you came back to fight with a force that you never knew where it came from, your mind was a great tool to be impossible, the possible. You are unique in the world, the world will one day know about you, because you are an individual who decided to change his life 360 degrees in a positive way to transcend forever.

Decide to change the world, starting with what belongs to you, you have countless technological tools that connect you to the globalized world, if you use all the tools that belong to you with intelligence, you will achieve your goals causally, the cause and effect that manifests in your extraordinary life, will be a priority for your development, always be hungry for knowledge, always focus on learning, turn around, get the magnificent experience that over time will become wisdom, use all your senses, love with force, fall in love with your projects of your life itself, be aware that you are in this wonderful world for a reason.

Your courage manifest it in your creations, in your decisions, adversity will be a complement to always appreciate what you have or what you have obtained, always be grateful for the minimum you receive, abundance will come to your life in a natural way, if you start to appreciate the wonderful things that surround you your fabulous life will surprise you, it is the only life you have, there is no other, live it to the fullest, with a great responsibility focused on creativity and innovation, without expecting to receive anything in return, do it with a lot of love, when you least expect it the great reward will touch the door of your heart.

There is a great call at the world level, where we are looking for leaders ready to face any challenge that comes their way, these great leaders must think about humanity, the great synergy that unites the brilliant minds, it is a great light that communicates with the universe, the positive thoughts, are links that form organizations, communities, countries with a great strength that exemplify, the environment with a fabulous doctrine of how things should be done, so that they transcend forever the future generations.

Join the team of winners, change your thinking, show your strengths, dare to face the challenges that arise, think like the great leaders of all times, that suffering, storms made them stronger, every step, I form a great meaning in their lives, the total surrender in each moment, it was the unique identification with the universe, your power of development must be maintained before the worst obstacles that arise, your initiative must be focused on transcending forever.

¨To reach success, you have to go through unpredictable ways, you will find darkness, storms, barriers, which will impede your path, it depends on you if you accept the great challenge¨, it is important to analyze our paths in life, when we obtain things in a easy, we do not feel any feeling for having achieved them, instead when we fight, we fight constantly, to achieve our goal, it is recorded in our minds, all the storms that we have, the effort made in our subconscious is something we will never forget, we have So much appreciation for the goal achieved, because we almost gave our lives to enjoy the pleasure of having the most precious thing that led us to the realization, value what you have with a special force, so that you always find abundance in your path, success it is not easy to achieve, for this reason, when it knocks on our door, all those expressed emotions appear throughout life, appreciate what you have with strength and determination.

¨The solutions are not easy to achieve, but when several brilliant minds are united, with the same objective, a dream can come true¨, so that a dream becomes reality, it takes a lot of work, perseverance, total dedication, love to what what you do, give much more, strive to the maximum day to day, to achieve your goals, is a great structure, when you join a group of positive and brilliant minds, can create great solutions, before any project, great synergy, play a fundamental role, where the impossible can be made possible, every initiative that shows, a great effort, work, dedication, carries great results, that will be appreciated forever, because in the dark, where nobody found an alternative, appeared by Magic art, the great miracle of making a dream come true.

"Being a warrior, it's easy to say, but putting on your armor, going out to explore the world, with great determination, to seek and take advantage of the opportunities that arise, are the beginnings of a great battle", the decision you have made, is your property, you have the free will to choose, whatever you like, there is a great global menu of alternatives, where you can choose, the way you want, there are easy roads that anyone can travel or there are complicated ones, unique and incomparable, that can only be the warrior attitudes, where they will demand the best of you, your maximum effort, even more, to simply achieve a desired difference, if you want to be a great warrior, fight with all your strength, show why You are in this wonderful world, to be the best, you are willing to leave your mark on your path, with decision delivery and great creativity.

¨Everyone in the world, we have great potential, you just have to do the great task, to find that great treasure you crave¨, it is not easy, but that wonderful way is easy, if you ask for the best, you must be willing to offer a lot more than the best, increase your skills, take the initiative to do what you propose of the best quality, so you do not have to do it again, a treasure is hard to find, if it were easy, anyone would be rich in the world, your initiatives have to be enriching, so you find all the tools, hidden in your great potential, when you discover those hidden strengths, you are amazed, because you never imagined that they belonged to you, explore, at any moment you can find the great surprise, that You have found a world, fantastic, different from the one you were used to, take advantage of the great gifts that the wonderful life gives you.

" Fight constantly, never give up, every step you take, with energy, determination, at any moment can knock on your door, a great miracle ", life demands that if you want to fulfill your dreams, you must be willing to work to the maximum, with discipline, spirituality and love, sometimes when you do not find a way out, a great response appears that illuminates your mind, your heart, most people in the world, have witnessed or commented on a miracle , miracles exist, but they demand the best of you, offer more than necessary, by changing your life, by the great path of constant light, of realization, of joy, of great happiness, you have the great decision , dare to look for new results, that give a meaning to your life, that give you the great initiative, that identifies you forever, that you have the courage to face any challenge that comes your way.

"To be spiritual, is a great achievement, to face any challenge that is present, it is also a support base for the great construction, which you think to create", in what you believe it is important that you manifest your emotions, your true feelings, there is something wonderful that surrounds us, that has created the magnificent things that are around us, in times of catastrophes, extreme crises, spiritual power, is a light of breath that penetrates our mind, our soul and our great heart, when you are spiritual , you know that miracles exist, when you do not observe any remedy, solution to your problems, the spiritual being connects you with the fantastic universe, taking you on the path of great realization.

¨The feedback, is important for the development of any project, for the great realization of your life itself, take what comes to your life with great appreciation¨, constantly modify your life, with positive interests, it is important, each system needs to improve day by day, what you take depends on you, each new experience complements you, leads you over time to great wisdom, any project, where countless people participate, creates a synergy that is manifested, in the achievement of objectives , when you become a great explorer, you are attentive to what is happening around you, you are alert to the big and small events that invade you, to be awake before the knowledge, it is a great alternative that focuses on the constant development, each firm step that present, will be reflected, on the way to your goals and goals.

An idea can lead you to a great path, a set of ideas can lead you to build your life and the people involved, be receptive to what happens around you, show you a different path than what you are used to, a great idea, it can take you to the road of construction, dare to dream, to look for alternatives, to provide you with the necessary tools, dare to experiment, do not be afraid to make some mistake, infinity of realizations in the world, have started with an idea , where the trial and error, were part of them, decide today is the time to start, if you have an idea, start working, perform the necessary practices, to know the effectiveness, complements, organizes, dare to start with decision, strength, hunger for great knowledge, you do not know maybe you have one of the best ideas in the world.

¨Has what you like, work on what you like, have strength, perseverance, with great love, what complements your life¨, dedicate yourself to the work you are in love with, feel that you could do it without receiving an incentive, of course you will always receive something economic, because we all have this kind of needs, but when you mentalize in this way, you have the ability to do what you propose with enjoyment, enthusiasm, love, doing what you like should be a great goal in your life. life, because you only live once, you must do it to the fullest, as if it were the last day of your existence, when you enjoy what you do life is pleasant, life is unique, special, knocks at your door the great miracle that illuminates your soul and your heart, the fantastic happiness.

Atrévete a soñar, todas las grandes innovaciones en el mundo, ¨Take the positive options that life gives you, they may only appear once in your path¨, when you are attentive to what is happening around you, you have a fabulous perception that focuses on your goals, sometimes there are big gifts that appear in our life, from us depends the appreciation, the appreciation of every detail, to receive the great options that give us the opportunity, to know a different panorama, to be enriched by new experiences, to create new tools, that allow us to develop, new strategies, which complement our path, towards realization.

¨It is important that you value the past in an intelligent way, taking the great experiences, because the future does not belong to you, you are the owner of the magnificent present, today is the great day to begin¨, you can not live in the past and be constantly dreaming of the future, the real place, where you must use all your strengths, everything you have, is in the fantastic present, is the only place that belongs to you, each step you take, do it firmly, with great determination, to be willing to fight to achieve your goals, today is the most important day of your life, take advantage of the scenario that belongs to you, to take your maximum potential, keep in mind that every day is different, the great experiences you got in the past, you should use in the present, complementing them as great tools, that will facilitate your understanding of the challenges that surround you, today is the most important day of your life, what you do must do it with perseverance, love, spirituality, using the maximum effort, to observe your wishes come true.

¨ There is a world call, where leaders are asked, willing to give life itself, for their ideals, for their transforming power¨, every project, every initiative, requires leadership, discipline, a great commitment, everything focused towards construction, having a strong structural foundation, that supports any creation, is a great beginning, towards the transformation of projects, ideas, where the leader creates a union of brilliant minds, with the aim of facing the storms, barriers, obstacles that arise, to inhabit the most complicated road, the great road that requires the maximum effort, the great path of the winners.

¨ Open your mind to knowledge, get new experiences, be enriched by the alternatives that transform, the only thing that can avoid your growth and development, is death¨, you have a fabulous menu of alternatives, but there will also be great barriers to avoid your path , it depends on you to use the necessary tools, to go out in search of success, every road you walk is full of new things, great unique experiences, there will be many obstacles, you will suffer, spectacular storms, but your positive mentality will give you the great courage to continue forward, you know that the only thing that can stop you in this wonderful life, is to die and you are not afraid because you know that all the people in the world are exposed to that sad reality, the only remedy you have is to live each time lapse that belongs to you the most, with the great dream, goal of being happy.

Mission, eliminate world poverty, is one of many projects created in the world, to find an existential reason, to benefit countless people, to observe an invaluable treasure that is a sincere smile, when projects are created that come from the heart, they are sincere initiatives, that move minds, souls, love is present with a great indescribable sensation, there is a great light, that eliminates any darkness, loses the notion of time, fatigue disappears, there are infinity of strategies, where the personal growth, the synergy of several minds, joins to make a single project, benefit the world, go down in history as a great project, which has a spiritual connection with the universe, is a construction that nobody can stop, because it was formed with true feelings, with great work, enthusiasm, perseverance, courage, a great and beautiful love.

They have started with a dream, do not have limits, you have your property, that magnificent dream that comes from the depths of your heart, express your emotions to the fullest, enjoy the great wonderful moments that come to your life, be forever grateful , for the minimum that you receive, take it as if it were a great prize, it flows through the current of your life, there will be obstacles, impressive barriers, that impede your way, look for strategies, alternatives, do not stop, you come to this wonderful world to deliver the best of you, your life is the great stage that belongs to you, ask for the best in life, but dare to offer more of the best, that sometimes feel faint, for the great efforts you make, feel a pride, It will be an exemplary light that illuminates you forever and that overcomes you to illuminate future generations, with your great mark of creativity, innovation and something that is the basis of your life, the fantastic love.